LIFE AND WORK AMONG
THE NAVVIES.

1. The Welland Viaduct and part of group of huts at Seaton yard.
2 The line in course of construction.   3. Brick-making machine; Pits on Tunnel.

LIFE AND WORK

AMONG

THE NAVVIES.

BY

D. W. BARRETT, M.A.,

VICAR OF NASSINGTON;
LATE CURATE IN CHARGE OF THE BISHOP OF PETERBOROUGH'S
RAILWAY MISSION.

SECOND EDITION.

London:
WELLS GARDNER, DARTON & CO.
PATERNOSTER BUILDINGS.
1880.

REV THE CANON D. W. BARRETT

The Reverend Daniel William Barrett was a 25-year-old bachelor when, in 1876, he was called by the Bishop of Peterborough to the newly formed Bishop of Peterborough's Railway Mission. Prior to this appointment, Barrett was a graduate of Trinity College, Dublin, where he attained his BA in 1871. He became curate of Bierley, West Yorkshire, in 1872, and from 1873 to 1876 was the curate of Waltham-in-the-Wolds, Leicestershire. During this time he attained his MA. It was from Waltham that he took up the difficult challenge presented by the Bishop's Mission, which is recounted in this book, *Life and Work Among the Navvies*.

In December 1878 the Railway Mission was drawing to a close, as various aspects of the heavy work reached completion, and he was then licensed to the parish of Lyddington, Rutland, a living that had fallen on hard times. Though he was there but a few months, under his care great improvements were made, both to the spiritual life of the parish and to the church building. While at Lyddington he became Secretary of the Navvy Mission Society. In June 1879 he was appointed to the living of Nassington-cum-Yarwell, Northamptonshire. That same year *Life and Work Among the Navvies* was published to great acclaim, and eventually ran to four editions. He was at Nassington until 1887, and during that time was Rural Dean of Oundle, Northamptonshire. From 1887 to 1910 he was Rector of Chipping Barnet, and was also Chaplain of Chipping Barnet Union from 1889 to 1909, Rural Dean of Barnet from 1893 to 1909, and Honorary Canon of St Albans from 1905 to 1910. His work *Sketches of Church Life* was published in 1902. In 1910 he became Rector of All Saints, Holdenby, Northamptonshire, and there he remained until his death in September 1928. He was the author of several successful works, including *The Royal Prisoner of Holdenby*.

On 25 July 1877, during his ministry to the Kettering to Manton navvies, he married Annie Sophia, daughter of Captain Rendell RN. There were two sons and two daughters. Canon Barrett is buried in Holdenby churchyard, beside his wife, who predeceased him by two years.

J. Ann Paul, 2003

The portrait of Rev D. W. Barrett is reproduced by permission of Rev C. Goble.

First published in 1879
This facsimile edition first
  published 2003

British Library Cataloguing in
  Publication Data

A catalogue record for this book is
  available from the British Library.

ISBN 1 85794 213 2

Silver Link Publishing Ltd
The Trundle
Ringstead Road
Great Addington
Kettering
Northants
NN14 4BW

Tel/Fax: 01536 330588
email:
  sales@nostalgiacollection.com
Website:
  www.nostalgiacollection.com

Printed and bound in Great Britain

A Silver Link book
from
The NOSTALGIA *Collection*

Dedication.

TO MESSRS LUCAS AND AIRD.

GENTLEMEN,—

In allowing me to dedicate to you this sketch of " Life and Work among the Navvies," you confer a special favour on me.

Your kind permission gives me an opportunity of expressing publicly, what I have often done in private, my grateful acknowledgment of your keen desire and generous efforts to ameliorate the social condition, and still better, to further the spiritual interests, of the men in your employ.

This is not the expression of my own feelings merely ; it is an echo of the sentiment of hun-

dreds of your subordinates, ranging from the leading members of your staff down to your humblest
workmen.

That others in your position may recognise, as
you have so nobly done, their true relation as
masters to their men, and show a like regard
to the claims and blessings of Christianity, by
furthering the mission of our National Church, is
the prayer of

Your grateful and obliged servant,

THE AUTHOR.

NASSINGTON VICARAGE, WANSFORD,
November 1879.

INTRODUCTORY NOTE.

THIS little sketch is written with several objects in view. One is to supply a record of a special undertaking in railway work, and an account of the manners and customs of the "navvies," and railway labourers in general, who are employed in making new lines. Another is to call attention to some interesting and encouraging features of the work of the Church amongst them.

The writer has a still more definite object than either of these, and in the hope of attaining it he has adopted a style, for which perhaps he ought to apologise to his more cultured reader. It is hoped that this book may fall into the hands of numbers of workmen on our great public works, and it is therefore addressed to them, in many places, in such terms as, it is thought, will be most likely to attract and influence them.

That such suggestions as are thrown out will be taken kindly is not doubted, and it is earnestly hoped that some permanent good may, by these means, be effected. The author has hardly the right to claim much originality either of thought, matter, or expression. He gratefully acknowledges that he has received most valuable help from many sources. Amongst others he wishes to name Messrs. Lucas & Aird, Barlow, Sons, & Baker, A. C. Priestley, R. Stannard, A. Stannard, C. J. Wills, P. N. Meares, J. Bruster, J. White, W. Chapman, T. G. Jones, B. C. Caffin, T. A. Walker, T. Acland.

To many of the foremen and workmen, including not a few navvies whose names are unmentioned, he owes a debt of acknowledgment. Specially to Messrs. S. Hilling, H. Plowman, J. Price, J. Shelley, D. Juett, W. Curtis, J. H. Froggatt, T. Knight, J. Reynolds; and to Mr. C. Drake, for photographs.

There are others who must not be omitted. The Author's thanks are also due to the " Navvy Mission Society," for a report of its proceedings and much valuable help; to Mrs. C. Garnett; to the Rev. A. J. Ingram, of the Additional Curates' Society, for the gift of some valuable blocks for the purpose of illustration; and to the Editor of the " Grantham Journal," for records of interesting events.

CONTENTS.

Part I.

CHAPTER I.

THE START.

CHAPTER II.

PROGRESS OF THE WORK.

CHAPTER III.

STATISTICS.

CHAPTER IV.

HERE AND THERE ON THE LINE.

Part II.

CHAPTER I.

WHAT IS A NAVVY?

CHAPTER II.

NAVVY SLANG.

CHAPTER III.

NICKNAMES.

Part III.

CHAPTER I.

INTRODUCTORY.

CHAPTER II.

NOTES OF PROGRESS.

CHAPTER III.

RED LETTER DAYS.

CHAPTER IV.

LEISURE EVENINGS.

CHAPTER V.

A LETTER.

CHAPTER VI.

THE EXODUS.

APPENDICES.

LIFE AND WORK AMONG THE NAVVIES.

PART I.

CHAPTER I.

THE START.

A GLANCE at an ordinary railway map will soon show the object the promoters of the Kettering and Manton Railway had in view, when they determined to add one more avenue to the closely-tangled mesh of iron roads which already intersect our country. A more direct and expeditious route from the North to London was desired; and several companies had, in years gone by, surveyed the district lying between Nottingham and Kettering, with the view of forming a connecting line with their respective systems; but it was not till 1874, and then only after difficulty and opposition, that a Bill was obtained by the enterprising directors of the Midland Company, and the line finally decided on. What were several hundred thousands of pounds, or even, if necessary, a few millions, in order to shorten the distance, when other lines were competing in the race to London? The route from Carlisle could be lessened by about thirty-five miles, and the work must be done. This little book professes to tell, in plain and ordinary language, how the scheme was carried out, something about the men who did it, and what the Church tried to do for them.

Before attempting to enter more fully on the plan we have marked out, let us take a trip through the district to which this account specially refers, the district, I mean, lying between Kettering on the Midland main line and Manton on the line from Leicester to Peterborough. The new line, which will henceforth be the Midland great highway, begins at Nottingham and runs to Melton-Mowbray, so well known to the disciples of Nimrod. Here it falls in with the old branch to Peterborough, over which the traveller proceeds as far as Manton, where the second section of the undertaking has its point of departure. The description of the Nottingham and Melton portion of the railway must be left to other hands. It is at Manton where our special work begins. Starting from thence, we will give a general sketch as we go. The line, the first half-mile or so, runs along an embankment averaging five and thirty feet high, by the valley of the Chater, Wing church and village lying away on the hill-top to the left. The line then suddenly pierces two ridges of hill lying between the villages of Preston on the right and Wing on the left. After running underground for about a quarter of a mile it emerges into a deep cutting, and passes along a low embankment to the larger tunnel at Glaston. From this embankment a view of Preston and Uppingham churches may be obtained by looking up the valley to the west and south-west. The tunnel at Glaston is over a mile long, and when you get once more into the daylight, a glimpse of the Welland valley is obtained as you pass along the steep embankment,

which carries you over the fields to the mouth of a third
tunnel, which pierces the spur of the high land jutting out
from Seaton village to the valley just mentioned; this
tunnel is a very short one, and as you come out at the south
end the whole Welland vale lies stretched out before you.
As you cross it by the magnificent viaduct over-topping
Harringworth spire, the Gretton hillside is reached, and
skirting this, with Gretton lying above you and half a
dozen villages or so dotted over the plain below, you come
to the high bank which is to convey you to a fourth
subterranean cavern, under the wooded heights of Rockingham Castle and Corby. This tunnel brings you a
mile farther on your journey, and, when you leave it
behind, you find yourself at once in the deepest cutting
of the line, with its iron-stone walls bounding its course
a mile or so farther, till you reach Corby village. Here
the bolder features of the Rutland hills tame down into
the more richly wooded and gentle slopes, and you travel
along one or two more steep banks, cross Harper's Brook
and the river Ise by two small viaducts, and finally run
on to the old main line through another iron-stone
cutting about a mile south of the Rushton station. This
is only a very general description of the route, which
is about fifteen and three-quarter miles in length. The
principal landowners through whose property it passes are
the Duke of Buccleuch, Sir W. de Capell Brooke, Lady
Cardigan, Lord Winchelsea, Colonel Tryon, the Marquis of
Exeter, Lord Lonsdale, the Hon. W. C. Evans Freke, the
Rev. Chas. Boys, E. P. Monckton, W. C. Thornhill, and
W. Sheild, Esqs. Besides these there are sundry owners
of smaller properties whose domains have been intersected
in the various villages. The names of the owners of these
properties I have been unable to ascertain.

In the spring and early summer of 1875, a survey of
the line was made by the Midland Company's engineers,

C. B. Baker, Esq., and Crawford Barlow, Esq., of the eminent firm of Barlow, Son, and Baker, civil engineers. It was from this survey that the working plans were ultimately drawn out. The work was entrusted to the well-known contractors, Messrs. Lucas and Aird, who carried it through from the beginning to the end, having entered on their task in the month of June, in the same year in which the survey was made. There was no ceremony of turning the first sod, at least publicly; but I am told that Mr. Cuthell and a few others did informally inaugurate the undertaking at the Rushton cross roads. On account of the magnitude of the scheme, and the difficult nature of the country through which the line had to pass, the amount of plant was exceedingly large, and overtaxed the transit resources then at the command of the local railway stations; for, notwithstanding the haulage along the country roads of huge engines, ponderous waggons, and various kinds of gearing required for sinking the tunnel shafts, these stations were constantly blocked up with the sudden influx of traffic. By and by the platforms at Manton, Seaton, Rockingham, and other local stations, began, as some of the much-vexed stationmasters could tell you, to present a very busy and sometimes perplexing scene. Navvies, with their wives and families, might be seen standing in little knots discussing the route, or crowding round the officials asking their way to the new line. Huge bundles of bedding, boxes of household stuff, sundry articles of furniture of all kinds, bedsteads, frying-pans, bird cages, perambulators, clocks, chairs, and other things " too numerous to mention," arrived by every train.

As soon as the work had fairly started, men crowded in from all parts of the country, and the question had to be solved where the new-comers were to be lodged. It was clear that they were too many for the villages lying near, though hundreds took shelter there. The difficulty, however, was only temporary, and it was soon settled. The work had to be done, there must be men to do it, and they must have homes to dwell in. Soon the hills and dales, for fifteen miles, began to echo with the sound of the mattock, the hammer, and the axe. Hut villages seemed to grow up like mushrooms. Taking your stand on any one point of the line above ground, I do not think there was a single spot from which you could not see a hut, or the smoke of it anyhow, rising from one of the little chimneys and curling up in faint blue wreaths from some snug nook, where the humble home was hidden by a dip in the landscape. Over two hundred of these erections were made, mostly of wood, a few of bricks, and some even of sods of earth. Here stood a cluster of six on the roadside; there a group of fifty or so, across the hill-top; nestling down in the valley there, by the river-side, half a hundred more; again, a little colony in the midst of the woods, of which and its settlers you could catch a glimpse through the open "riding." Here and there they stood in their quaintly attractive picturesqueness all along the line. Presently we will look at them a little closer. To come back to prosy particulars, let us chronicle the exact spot where they stood. Many who take up this book will be glad to see a record of their exact locality, for by the time this reaches the reader's eye, they will, in all probability, be swept away, and the grass be growing green and luxuriant over the spot on which they stood. Coming from Manton station and travelling on towards Kettering, you would have passed groups of them opposite the Chater Viaduct, on Wing cross-roads, along the valley to the tunnel, and on Glaston hill-side. Seaton hill was crowned with a cluster known as "Cyprus." In the Welland valley on the Seaton side was another settlement. Some few were scattered all along by Gretton; on the borders of Corby Wood was quite a

Canadian forest scene in the busy camp which had been formed there. Smaller lots were erected at Penn Green, Thorny Lane, Harper's Brook, and the cross roads at Rushton. Very picturesque they all looked, and many a pleasant half hour have I spent under many of their roofs in friendly converse with the inmates.

No sooner were the hut villages erected, and the plant on the ground, than, to use a military phrase, " an attack was made along the whole line ;" and it will be our business in the next chapter to describe how the charge was conducted.

CHAPTER II.

PROGRESS OF THE WORK.

Now for a busy scene. There were soon signs in plenty of active operations. The line was staked out, the huts were up, the material was collected, some of the men were there, and many more on their way; only leaders were wanted to put things in motion. A local agent was at once appointed by the contractors to represent them, and superintend the whole work of construction. James Eagle, Esq., was selected for the post, and he retained it till the spring of 1877, when he was succeeded by R. Stannard, Esq., who conducted affairs till the completion of the line. The course was mapped out into four chief districts, extending north and south from Glaston, Seaton, Corby, and Rushton. Over these, other agents were placed in charge, with less or more independency of action, but at the same time responsible to the chief representative of the firm, who was appointed as manager over the whole. The several agents were—for Glaston district, Mr. C. J. Wills; for Seaton, Messrs. Clegg, Hughes, and Wills; for Corby, Mr. White; for Rushton, Messrs. Roberts and Blue. Under these, again, were various sub-officers almost too numerous to mention, clerks, time-keepers, inspectors, store-keepers, gangers, foremen, and a host of others all rendering valuable aid in carrying out the scheme.

Gretton, being the central village on the line, was

the general " rendezvous " of the various officials of all
grades. Here was the chief engineering office, presided
over, in the earlier stage of the works, by A. C. Priestley,
Esq., A.I.C.E., with a staff of clerks and draughtsmen at
command. The cashier department was first in charge
of Mr. William Thomson, and then of Mr. T. G. Jones,
who must have paid away many tens of thousands of
pounds. Gretton was also the centre for the engineers
of the company; these were represented there by Crawford Barlow, Esq., C.E., who again, like the contractors,
had his representative authorities scattered up and down
the works.

When the staff was complete, and the men at hand,
the first serious work was begun by sinking a deep shaft
into the bowels of the earth near Corby Wood, in order to
commence the tunnel there. The various sections of the
undertaking were let to sub-contractors, whose names
were legion, one undertaking a cutting here, another an
excavation there, a third a bridge over a stream, a fourth
a roadway arch, and so on from one end to the other.

The work proceeded rapidly, one scarcely knew how.
In a very few months a very ugly scratch was drawn
across the face of the country, hill-sides were scooped
out, piles of clay began to appear like huge mole-banks
in the fields over the tunnels, masses of brickwork were
seen rising out of the ground, steam engines, with their
appendages of trucks, were to be heard frantically rattling
up and down the slopes and over the temporary wooden
bridges, or rushing rapidly along the rough iron ways laid
down to carry the materials. Here and there the embankments began to stretch out their rugged sides into the
pleasant fields through which they had to pass. The
jingling chains of the gaily ribboned tip-horse, the merry
whistle of the tipper, cut short by the heavy thud of the
waggon stopped suddenly at the bank head, kept sounding

all along. These were varied by the sharp clink-aty-clink
of the trowel, and the resounding "Holloa! Compo!!"
from the banksman at the pit's mouth, as he shouted out
his warning to his mate below. All was hurry-scurry
and bustle. "Now, my lad! shift that muck" (dirt), was
the frequent exhortation of the ganger as he stood in the
cutting or on the bank, and caught an idler resting on his
shovel or leaning on his pick. Who can forget the scene
at night, with the watch-fires glaring far and near in the
darkness, as they lit up the sky with an aurora-like flame,
or crackling, as the wind fanned their sparks through the
chilly air and lent to the faces of the passers-by a wan
and ghastly hue? Or who can forget the miners' shout,
"Lower out! Riders!!" as they called to the man at
the wheel to let them down below for their spell of mid-
night toil? The glare of the forge, where the stalwart
sons of Vulcan wielded their heavy sledges, added one
more strange sight to the weird features of the night.
The flickering lamps of the workmen and watchers, as
they passed up and down on their respective errands,
lent their share of brilliancy to the streak of busy light.
Parodies, like comparisons, are odious, but the temptation
at the present moment is too great, and we must attempt
one description of the scene.

From Rushton end to Manton town, from Wing to Harper's Brook,
To nightly toil both men and boys right eagerly betook;
And bright in north, and bright in south, the glaring beacons stood,
High on the Gretton bank they shone, they shone from Corby Wood;
Far on the hills the trav'ller saw across the Rutland shire
Peak beyond peak, in dazzling blaze, those flashing sheets of fire;
The rustics left their flocks to roam by Seaton's grassy rills,
And now as miners throng'd to pierce red Glaston's claybound hills,
From Morcott's street and Preston's lanes the nightly toilers sped;
From Oakham town and Bisbrook slopes a motley throng was led.

This will give some fair idea of the activity displayed.

The sturdy little engine which stood down by the murmuring streamlet, and with a husky groan and laboured pulse forced the water into the tanks above, seemed to enter into it all, and to be as active as any of the men whose footsteps were hurriedly tramping over the wooden bridge under which it was placed. Even the very wheelbarrows as they rattled up and down the chain-falls, with their loads of bricks or earth, added their note of harmony to the tune. Look at that powerful fellow on the bank there, "Tommy Tough-back;" see how he tugs away at that iron bar, till down tumbles a mass of clay, which has no sooner reached the gang below than with pick and spade, eager as a pack of foxhounds at the death, they divide the spoil. Yonder go the loud rumbling trucks with the fragments to the tip-head. There, too, is "Billy Thick-leg" standing on the buffer. "Look out, Billy, or they'll be off the metals, and your heels will be in the air." All right, my man, you are over the points now, stick to it. Bump! bump!! bump!!! now they stand, and one by one they deposit their crumbling load down the rough slope. Look ahead there, half a mile farther on. A puff of smoke, a dull thud, a shower of earth, and stones flying through the air, show that a mine has sprung. A score of hands are busy at once consigning the broken masses to the waggons standing by.

Then just go and lean on that bridge and look up the cutting there at that hive of human bees, each securing and carrying off his load. Chip! chip!! chip!!! there stands the stonemason, chisel and hammer in hand; that coping-stone will soon be rounded off and in its place. Clang! clang!! clang!!! the sounding metals ring again in the crisp and frosty air, as the platelayer drives home his "metal dogs" into the sleepers below. The harsh screech of the revolving saw, as it rips up the rough timber and sends its cloud of dust into the air, is another sign of the eager push. Keeping tune with all this is the continuously rumbling rattle of the twirling pan, from which the well-ground· mortar is supplied to the men of brick and stone. All these sights and sounds show you how the work progresses—work by day, and work by night. Here a little and there a little soon work a change. But this is above ground.

Go and step into that "skip" which hangs quivering in the iron bond over the pit's mouth. Now for a trip through damp and misty air rising up from beneath; down you go one hundred and fifty feet below.

> "Out you jump,
> Mind the sump."

Light your lamp from that flickering candle which sticks in the clay there, and away you go. Look up into the heading. There's a busy gang. Clink of trowel again, thrust of spade, ring of hammer, smell of powder, rattle of trolly, shout of runners in and out, lights flickering up and down, soon tell how the work goes on. Oh! who wouldn't be a navvy, and enjoy the merry rattle of a busy and useful life? Such life has its sorrows and its wrongs, but it has withal an aspect attractive, bright, and free. As time creeps on, mine creeps on towards mine, the faint knocks of the miners' picks are heard with increasing loudness as they strike away at the narrowing mass which separates them and their mates on the other side. Now the heading is driven, rough hand grasps hand, and the work goes right merrily along. No wonder that Pit No. 2 soons opens out to No. 1, and No. 1, again, with its dark eyeball, Cyclops-like, glares on the open fields around. No wonder that the ugly mounds of clay above increase, and the light of heaven soon shines from end to end through the once dark mass underground. Three years ago that long roll which hung on the office

wall showing the progress of the work, was crossed here
and there by only a few faint lines of red, but week by
week the lines widened into long patches of colour, till
they became blended into one harmonious whole.   For
many a long month huge loads of timber, coal, lime,
powder, picks, and iron might be seen hurried along the
route ; these grew less and less in number as the demand
grew smaller, and soon, instead of the rattle of the tip-
waggon, the clank of the metals might be heard as
they were fitted to their places on the newly-made road.
So day by day went by, the work decreased, the workmen
vanished, and a way was at length opened up for the
great Iron Horse.

CHAPTER III.

STATISTICS.

To general readers, I suppose, a chapter on statistics will prove, what the "navvy" too often says he is, "very dry;" but I will try and make it as readable as I possibly can; so please do not shut up the book in disgust, or skip what may prove really interesting. It is not in my power to make it particularly amusing, but I may perhaps succeed in making the account readable. Any way, it may attract attention to the fact that not the least of England's great industries at enormous expenditure of wealth and human sinew, is to be found often in out-of-the-way places, in the construction of our great iron roads. To begin with the flesh and blood power. The late Rev. L. M. Evans, who has recently taken considerable pains to arrive at a fair estimate of the number of men employed in public works, such as railways, reservoirs, docks, &c., says in an appeal lately issued on behalf of the "Navvy Mission Society":—

"What these needs are will perhaps be best understood from the following statement:—

"Inquiries recently addressed to the managers of large public works gave these results:—Replies were received from 34 places. The total number of men employed in these was 13,244. In 22 places out of the 34 the men were lodged in huts, because no other accommodation could be found for them sufficiently near to their work. The average number of huts in each place was 38; the average number of men employed nearly 400.

· "Out of the 34 places four only were found where a Sunday service
was held for the navvies, or attended by them. Only two places
were heard of which possessed a Sunday-school; three had night-
schools, and three day-schools for the children.

"But the total number of public works in progress in England is
much greater than 34—it is probably not less than 100; and the
total number of men employed may be roughly estimated at 40,000.
These, together with women and children, represent from 50,000
to 60,000 souls, to whose necessities we seek to minister."

Of this number the population of the Kettering and
Manton Railway formed no inconsiderable portion. Whilst
upon this subject of flesh and blood I may give a quotation
made by the Dean of Ripon, in a paper read before the
Church Congress at Sheffield, prefacing it by a remark of
his own. "When, therefore, a contractor undertakes a
great work of this description, he must find men who have
been trained to very hard and rough labours, who possess
physical qualities of health, muscular strength and endurance, who will not be afraid of exposure to inclement
weather when they are at work, of inhabiting a hut or shanty
on some moor or mountain side far away from the comforts
of social life. Take, for example (he adds), the following
extract from the interesting life of Mr. Brassey :—' The
labour which a navvy performs exceeds in severity almost
any other description of work—a full day's work consists
of fourteen sets a day (a set is a number of waggons,
in fact, a train). There are two men to a waggon. If a
waggon goes out fourteen times, each man has to fill seven
waggons in the course of a day. Each waggon contains
two and a quarter cubic yards. The result is that each
man has to lift nearly twenty tons' weight of earth on a
shovel over his head into a waggon. The height of the
lifting is about six feet. This is taking it at fourteen sets
a day, but the navvies contrive to get through sixteen
sets, and there are some men who will accomplish that
astonishing quantity of work by three or four o'clock

in the afternoon, a result, I believe, which is not nearly equalled by any other set of workmen in the world.'"

Let us come back to the Kettering and Manton line once more. It has been computed by those in a position to make an accurate statement on the subject, that the average number of men employed on the fifteen miles of railway was, for one year, upwards of 2500 (and for a few weeks even 3500). This includes the lodgers and others who walked in from the villages round. The number of huts was as follows:—Glaston district 70, Seaton 47, Gretton 12, Corby 50, Rushton 26, making a total of 205. The total annual rental would be something like £2000, but against this must be placed the cost of construction, drainage, and repairs. If the huts had been built along both sides of a road in single file, each hut actually touching the end of the other (including the shanties), they would have formed a compact street of more than three-quarters of a mile in length. This, of course, would not adequately represent the idea of the length of little hut towns when all congregated. It would be more accurate if we were to picture a street about *two* miles long, allowing about the space of twenty or thirty feet between each hut. Now for the local hut population. Assuming seven men to a hut in the busy time, this would give a resident hut population, roundly speaking, of 1500 men, excluding those who dwelt in the "shanty." Now come women and children. In many of the huts were two women, in some three, though this latter was not a frequent occurrence. Computing a woman and a half to a hut, this would give 307. The children under sixteen years of age were very numerous, as those who took part in the various school festivals well remember. Taking the very low average of three and a half to a hut, this brings the number of children to close upon 700, making a grand total of 2500 odd, actually resident on

the works, besides those in "shanties." Add to this
another thousand or fifteen hundred lodging or living
in the neighbouring villages, and coming in daily to the
work, so that the railway brought about 4000 new-
comers all told. The staff was very numerous. In almost
every village along the whole course of the line either
lodgings or houses were taken for their accommodation.
No less than nine houses, and some of them large, were
rented by the Firm for this purpose. Whilst speaking of
population, I remember one case in which the occupants
of a hut numbered nineteen souls; father, mother, seven
children and ten lodgers. Scarlatina broke out, but the
authorities took prompt measures. The lodgers were
dismissed, and the disease was stayed before it ended in
any mortality. It is very difficult to calculate the number
of "casuals" employed for a day or two, sometimes only
for "a shift," and then passing on to some other works,
"turning up" periodically at various places on their
round; but these men were not the true navvies, only a
sort of camp-followers, whose room was much to be
preferred to their company.

A very rapid impetus was necessarily given to trade,
as nearly all the supplies were drawn from the towns
and villages lying near, so that prices soon went up. All
sorts of tradesmen were quickly on the spot. In the
early morning and late at night carts of all descriptions
might be seen standing by the roadsides, near the huts,
from the brewer's huge dray to the fishmonger's little
two-wheeled handbarrow. Hucksters, packmen, cheap-
Jacks, milkmen, bookhawkers, shoemakers, tailors; "like-
ness-takers" rapidly followed in the wake, and I am
afraid many of them, much to their discredit, used to
delight in Sunday trading.

Now for another batch of figures from averages taken
during one year in the busiest time. I give these figures,

as they show in some way the amount of trade which the
new-comers brought into the district. A certain amount
of beer, some one will say, was necessary. Granted, nevertheless the quantity consumed was something fearful,
30 gallons say, which is below the mark, to every hut
per week. In some cases, but very · rarely, no beer
was drunk ; in others even as much as 50 or 60 gallons
have been consumed. This computation of 30 gallons
a hut per week, again I say a very low average, would
give roughly a weekly average all along of 6000 gallons,
or, for the year, 312,000 gallons. Beer was usually
retailed in the huts at 3d. per pint. Thus we get a
yearly expenditure in the huts alone of £31,200.
Suppose we say the brewers were paid 14d. per gallon ;
that gives to them £18,200, leaving £13,000 profit to
be divided amongst 200 huts. After this, dare I touch
on spirits ? Half a gallon a week to every hut at £1
per gallon, whisky being the favourite beverage of this
class. This exceeds £5000, again, in *one* year, and
it does not include beer and spirits consumed in the
neighbouring villages and towns, by *bonâ fide* railway
operatives who lodged, or marketed, or spent their evenings
there. When I made this calculation I looked with
horror and astonishment at the figures, and said, " I can't
believe it ! " but a friend of mine remarked at once, " You
needn't be astonished, for I know that for many months
a single brewer's agent, in one district alone, used to send
back empty every week between 50 and 60 eighteen-
gallon casks. This was exclusive of *two* other brewers
who regularly brought supplies on the ground. I was
an eyewitness of this," my friend added, " over and over
again." Just fancy, in that street I pictured above, an
annual expenditure of £36,000, you may say £40,000,
for it is nearer the mark, for intoxicating drink !

Fresh meat represents a large figure too. Let us

B

continue our calculations. For each person living on
the work, great and small, short and tall, say, ¾ lb. of
meat a day, at 9d. per pound. This represents the sum
of something over £25,000 per annum, supposing one-
half to be beef, a quarter mutton, and the remaining
portion pork; and valuing an average ox when dressed
for the butcher's stall at £20, a sheep at £2, a pig
at £4, we get about 600 oxen, 3000 sheep, 1500 pigs.
What a drove of cattle!

We have not done yet. Perhaps the reader will say it
is time you had; but these statistics are far too interesting to withhold. Tea is an important item. Two ounces
for each person per week, there goes £2000. Coffee
about half as much in quantity. It would be simply
impossible to calculate the various articles of grocery and
provisions, which must have amounted to many thousands of pounds. The clouds of smoke which have gone
up from the fragrant weed involve a calculation which does
not by any means end in smoke. What did the tobac-
conists of the district divide between them? Give a man
an ounce per week, and you have at once about £1000.
I quote roundly a few other figures—

Pickles, a bottle a week to every hut, would be 10,400 bottles a year, at 10d. per bottle .	£400
Jam, 3 lbs. a week per hut, at 6d. . . .	780
Butter, 3 lbs. at 1s. 6d.	2340
Sugar, 8 lbs. at 3d.	1000
Potatoes, 3 stones at 1s.	1560
Ham and bacon, 20 lbs. per week at 8d., gives close on	7000
Bread, say 20 loaves at 4d., nearly . . .	3500
Milk, 7 quarts a week at 4d., over . . .	1200
Tinned fish, 2 tins a week at 8d., over . . .	600

Add these items together, and they come very little
short of £80,000. Tens of thousands besides are omitted
for provisions unmentioned, and no account whatever is

taken of clothes, boots and shoes, &c.; nor is the cost of maintenance of those non-resident on the works, though brought into the neighbourhood by them, included. There is little doubt that the hut population alone spent in the neighbourhood quite £100,000 in the busiest twelve months.

What about wages? Weekly, about £3500 was paid, or rather above £180,000 per annum, when the works were in full swing. Miners earned about £2 as a rule, though some, working overtime, got much more; bricklayers, £2, 10s. a week, or upwards, to £3 or £4; labourers, £1 to £1, 5s; mechanics, £1, 16s; foremen of each class getting about £3.

A very pretty little series of figures now falls to our lot to lay before you. There were 17 locomotive, 56 portable and stationary engines, making a total of 73, varying from 6 to 20 horse power. Mortar pans 26. Most of these were working day and night for many months. It has been calculated that the little pumping engine alone, which has been at work at Glaston tunnel for three years, day and night, has pumped 6700 gallons every twelve hours, or about 4,891,000 gallons of water annually. This engine supplied all the water needed for all purposes within a radius of one mile.

One hundred and twenty horses were kept at one time, besides a large number hired. Trucks, trollies, trowels by the score, picks, spades, shovels, and saws by the hundreds. Bricks by the million. Of course we cannot calculate to a brick; but an account has been kept of the bricks made on the works and those received from other brickyards. The number used in the course of construction, including bridges, tunnels, viaducts, has been close on 90 millions; about 75 millions having been made on the works. How far do you think these bricks would reach if they were laid out end for end in single file ?   About 12,784, or nearly 13,000 miles; rather more, that is, than half-way round the world.   Coals !   You might think that the demand for railways alone would soon exhaust the supply, when I tell you that over 80,000 tons have been used on the Kettering and Manton Railway since its commencement to the present time, close on three years. Say 16s. per ton, that's the way the money goes ! £64,000 in a lump.   Perhaps, the reader is nearly blinded with figures already, and he exclaims, What a nuisance to have lime thrown in my eyes ! Lime, in round numbers, 11,000 tons.   The amount of earth excavated in cuttings, tunnels, and foundations, comes to something like $2\frac{1}{2}$ millions of cubic yards.   Now, reckoning one shovelful to every $\frac{1}{2}$ cubic foot, this presents a nice little calculation resulting in 135 millions of shovelsful.   Ashlar work, 24,000 cubic feet; iron work, in this case exceedingly small, amounted only to 230 tons.   Number of rails, 15,350, or 61,400 yards of single line.   The rails are, Settle and Carlisle section, 82 lbs. to the yard, laid in chairs on cross sleepers, nine sleepers to a rail of 24 feet in length.   The chairs weigh 40 lbs. each.   The sleepers measure 9 feet by 10 inches by 5 inches.   If I continue these statistics to any greater length, I expect the reader will *rail* at me, *settle* down in his *chair*, and become a *sleeper* himself.

CHAPTER IV.

HERE AND THERE ON THE LINE.

FOR a line of such a short extent the number of "big things" in the shape of long cuttings, tunnels, embankments, and viaducts is exceedingly large. We propose to give from authentic sources some account of the nature of the more extensive features of the work, which is of the heaviest description. There is probably no country line in England in which so much work has been compressed in any equally continuous length. It is much to be compared to the well-known Settle and Carlisle line for difficulties in construction, but has been, I believe, very much more costly per mile than even that expensive undertaking.

In an introductory chapter we gave a cursory sketch of the course of the line starting from Manton station. We now reverse the order of march, and begin at the Kettering end.

The line commences in this direction at a point about two miles north of Kettering station and seventy-three and a half miles from London. After diverging from the old main line, the first important work to be noticed is the cutting through which it almost immediately passes. This cutting has a striking appearance, having a thick vein of iron-stone in it, which forms an almost perpendicular wall between the clay slope above and below it. The iron-stone is of the kind known as the "Northamptonshire ore." The total amount of material excavated

from this, which is known as the Glendon cutting, was
about 260,000 cubic yards, of which about 100,000 were
iron-stone.

After leaving this, the line is carried across a deep
valley by a very large embankment, in the middle of
which is a short viaduct, slightly over fifty feet high, having five 40-feet arches built to form a passage-way for
the little river Ise.

Thence, shortly after, it passes over the public way
at the Rushton cross roads by a very substantial iron
girder bridge, and enters another large cutting known
as Rushton cutting, from which about 200,000 cubic
yards of material were excavated. The stratum here is
of blue lias clay with chalky stones intermixed, a most
tenacious substance, which made the digging the most
difficult of all on the line.

After leaving this cutting we pass along by a very
low bank and a couple of shallow cuttings for about the
distance of a mile, until the first station is reached. This
is named Geddington station, though in the parish of
Little Oakley. From there the line ascends quickly
until the summit is reached, one and a half miles farther
on, passing first over a deep bank with a viaduct in the
centre fifty-five feet high, having twelve arches, each forty
feet span. Leaving this bank it enters next a deep
cutting about three-quarters of a mile long, to make
which it was found necessary to remove 270,000 cubic
yards of clay, the upper part being blue lias conglomerate,
and the lower a stiff yellow of the oolite series. After
passing on another long bank and over another public road
bridge, the line reaches the village of Corby, where there
is another neat station-house situated in the sixth cutting
on our journey.

After this the largest and most important cutting in
the whole length is reached. Here, again, we have, as in

the first cutting, iron-stone lying between strata of clay above and below. The total quantity of earth and rock excavated here was over half a million cubic yards. The length of it is one mile, fourteen chains, and the depth about fifty-six feet. More than half the material was run through a long tunnel, to form an embankment about two miles northward. As you approach the tunnel, there is on either side a substantial " retaining wall," of more than a furlong in length, built up to the under side of the iron-stone. These walls, of course, terminate at the tunnel face.

The tunnel was commenced November 1875, and completed January 1878, the first engine with a train of waggons passing through in February. The mining was carried on down ten shafts, the deepest being 110 feet. Six of them were filled up when the brickwork was finished, the remaining four being bricked round and left open for ventilation. The tunnel was built in 423 lengths or pieces, and required about 20,000,000 bricks, the brickwork being from three-quarters to one yard thick. The bricks were made at three yards, viz., Corby Wood, Corby, " Bainesfield," each producing when in full work about 100,000 weekly. Fresh air was supplied underground either by driving a heading, or by pumping it down the shafts by means of what is called a " Blow George," a revolving wheel worked by a stationary engine, and connected with a zinc pipe leading to the pit. As may readily be imagined, the construction of this tunnel was a work of no ordinary difficulty. Here will be a suitable place to record a few notes as to this section of the line, which consisted mainly of the tunnel and the last cutting work to which I have referred. At one time there were about 1000 men employed on this section alone, comprising brickmakers, bricklayers, blacksmiths, carpenters, fitters, miners, navvies, and labourers of all descriptions. There were no less than thirty engines of various sorts and sizes. Sixty-two huts were erected near here; hence this was one of the largest settlements, and here the men stayed for the longest period, owing to the heavy nature of the works.

Returning to the line at the mouth of the tunnel we have just left, we pass through another cutting with its retaining wall on the east side. Here 35,000 cubic yards of earth had to be moved. We next pass over the largest bank on the line, being fifty-five chains long, and averaging a depth of about twenty-three feet. This brings us to Gretton station, which, I suppose, we may consider the half-way house, whence we must start to view some further engineering difficulties and enterprises. Mounting another bank, with Gretton village lying above us, and passing by another small cutting and bank, we arrive at the entrance of Cresswell cutting, from which 163,000 cubic yards were excavated. The line along the Gretton hillside follows a slightly different course from that which was originally intended. Soon after the work was commenced here, it was found that it would be impossible to complete it on the original centre line without incurring enormous expense, as the whole hillside showed a decided tendency to slip down. Just close to Gretton village itself, where a most determined effort was made to carry out the original plan, some acres of ground came sliding down and destroyed all that had been done, besides making a large area of land comparatively useless. It was then decided to change the route, and carry the line farther away from the hill where the cuttings were to be made, and to bring it in closer, where embankments could be formed. This presented one of the difficult tasks of the undertaking.

By another bank and through what is known as the Harringworth cutting, the fourth station, named Harring-

worth, is reached, and now we come to one of the
wonders of the line, and I may say of the country. A
more detailed account of the noble viaduct which spans
the valley of the Welland will prove interesting: we give
it in the words of the press.

"The Grantham Journal" records the festivities in
connection with its near completion, and adds an account
of its construction. •

"A grand banquet was given by Messrs. Lorden and Holmes, two
sub-contractors for the Manton and Kettering branch of the Midland Railway, on Wednesday evening, the 17th inst., in a large
shed, tastefully decorated (near to the Seaton railway station and
the above viaduct), to celebrate the keying of the last of the
eighty-two arches of this magnificent structure on 5th inst.   Lieu-
tenant-Colonel Tryon, of Bulwick Hall, occupied the chair, and was
supported by Mr. Barlow, jun., Mr. Stannard, Mr. Brown (surgeon, Uppingham), Mr. Orford (Stamford), and about eighty of
the engineers, sub-contractors, and agents connected with the
line.   The vice-chair was occupied by the Rev. D. W. Barrett,
supported by Mr. J. Bruster, Mr. Kelly, &c.   The banquet, dessert,
wines, &c., were supplied by Mr. Clifton, of the Crown Hotel,
Stamford, which were splendidly served up, and gave great satisfaction.   After the chairman and vice-chairman had proposed the
usual loyal and patriotic toasts, Mr. Barlow, jun. (one of the
engineers of the line), and Mr. Stannard (agent for the contractors) spoke of the viaduct as one of the grandest and most perfect
pieces of work in the United Kingdom, and reflecting the greatest
credit upon the sub-contractors and every one engaged upon it.
Various toasts and songs occupied the evening until twelve o'clock,
when all dispersed with three times three cheers for Messrs. Lorden
and Holmes for their superb entertainment.   The Welland viaduct
crosses the Welland valley, from Harringworth to Seaton, in the
counties of Northampton and Rutland, and is one of the longest
structures of this kind in England, being three-quarters of a mile
in length.   It has eighty-two arches of forty feet span, some of
them sixty feet in height.   The eighty-one piers are six feet
thick, except ten, which are double thickness, and are called
'block piers,' to isolate the arches in sets, and prevent any under-
strain being continued indefinitely from arch to arch.   The
average height is fifty-seven feet above ground.   The foundations

of the piers and abutments are of concrete—some of them are of a considerable depth. The whole of the structure is erected with bricks manufactured on the ground, with Derbyshire gritstone springers, string-course, and coping ; the arches and spandrels are all covered with two coats of asphalt. The first brick was laid in March 1876, and the first arch was commenced in June 1877. It has been pushed on with such vigour that the arches were finished in the first week in July 1878. The work contains 20,000,000 bricks, 20,000 cubic yards of concrete, and 19,000 cubic feet of stone. Brickwork in lime, 37,543 cubic yards, in cement 5826 cubic yards. Barrow lime is used in the concrete and mortar throughout the whole work, supplied by Messrs. Ellis and Sons, Mount Sorrel, Leicester. Messrs. Barlow, Son, and Baker, London, are the engineers for the line, and their inspector of the works is Mr. G. W. Smith. The contractors for the whole of the works are Messrs. Lucas and Aird, London ; their agent on the works is Mr. Stannard ; Mr. W. H. Lorden is the sub-contractor for the brickwork, and Mr. R. Holmes is the brickmaker."

If the bricks in this viaduct were laid end to end one thick continuously, they would reach a distance of 2840 miles, or, they would, if laid out side by side, form a paved pathway five feet three inches wide, for a distance of 200 miles—*i.e.*, from London to York.

Casting a parting glance at the viaduct, we move on towards our destination at Manton. The next feature which strikes us is the network of lines converging at Seaton. We pass over, immediately after leaving the viaduct, a new line from Wansford to Seaton, and the old branch from Rugby to Stamford, and then enter another long cutting (150,000 cubic yards), which is divided into two sections by the Seaton tunnel, and is about ten chains in length, having been constructed to avoid the slips which seemed likely to give trouble if an open cutting were carried right through. Emerging from this, we are rapidly carried on a long bank to the Seaton viaduct of eight thirty-feet arches, rising to a rail level above ground of thirty-eight feet; and we see before us the great dark eyeball of Glaston tunnel, with smoky brow

frowning over the valley; but before we reach it, Glaston
cutting, from which 130,000 cubic yards of earth had to
be "shifted," must be traversed. Then the tunnel is reached.
This is the "second longest" tunnel on the entire route,
Corby tunnel being 1925 yards, and this 1846 yards,
thus giving Corby the advantage of 79 yards. If Corby
carries off the palm for length, Glaston is more remarkable for the engineering difficulties encountered in construction. The ground in many places proved excep-
tionally heavy, and the mining was consequently of an
exceedingly difficult and dangerous nature. The quantity
of timbering used was enormous. No less than 23,000
cubic feet of timber had to be built in with the brickwork,
as it could not be withdrawn in the usual way. Much
of the tunnel is lined with blue Staffordshire bricks to
resist the great crushing pressure; as the ordinary bricks
were in places reduced to powder, and therefore not
sufficiently strong to be used exclusively. Besides blue
bricks, something like 16,000,000 of ordinary bricks
were used in construction, which was very similar to
the tunnel at Corby, with the exception of the increased
difficulties. The scene of industry on the top of the
tunnel during its construction was a very striking one,
and has been described elsewhere. Our exit from underground brings us out through the fourteenth cutting,
55,000 cubic yards, on to a long bank running north-
wards, and takes us through Wing cutting, divided into
two sections by Wing tunnel. From the whole cutting
in both sides of the tunnel something like 135,000 cubic
yards were excavated. This tunnel is 16 chains in length,
and though short, it was by far the heaviest piece of underground work on the line, owing to the great weight from
the two huge over-pressing hills under the slopes of
which it has to pass, the valley between them not being

sufficiently shallow to admit of an open cutting throughout.

This tunnel is partially lined with "Staffordshire blues," and the brickwork is nearly three feet thick all through. As we come once more into the daylight, our telescopic journey is almost at an end, not, however, before mounting another embankment and crossing the Chater viaduct, which consists of five arches of 40 feet span, and has a rail level 42 feet above the ground. Here we draw up slowly, and find ourselves at the entrance of Manton station, where the line effects a junction with the branch from Leicester to Peterborough. From the starting-point at the Kettering end we have traversed a distance of 15¾ miles. It must have been noticed that our opening words at the head of this chapter have been verified. Let us take a summary view, and look back for details. In this short distance we have passed through sixteen cuttings, many of large extent, along twelve embankments, over one long, and three shorter viaducts, and dozens of bridges, through no less than four tunnels, two being over a mile in length. At one time, had you walked over the rough broken ground above and below, you might have seen at least 3500 workmen busy at the task of accomplishing what you now see finished.

Of the 15¾ miles, very nearly 3½ miles, which indicates little more than one-fifth of the whole line, is either in tunnel or on viaducts.

4. Head-gear of one of the Pits.
5. Wing Mission Chapel.
6. Turf huts: Navvies at work: Tip waggons.
7. Collection of Plant: Temporary buildings.
8. General view of country from Pit-head.

PART II.

CHAPTER I.

WHAT IS A NAVVY?

OPINIONS undoubtedly vary as to the description of this remarkable specimen of humanity. There is, however, not much doubt as to the manner in which he got his name, for the term "navvy" is simply an abridged form of the longer and less poetical word "navigator," which savours too much of the sound of "alligator" to be pleasant. And in fact, some people have a rough idea that the navvy is a sort of human alligator who feeds on helpless women and timid men, and frightens children into fits; the more so, because they have a remote idea of the connection of the navigators with the water of canals. If you had passed through the swampy fens of Lincolnshire a hundred years or so since, you would have seen many an "alligator"—I beg pardon, navigator—peeping out from the tall rushes, or else climbing the muddy bank of one of the marshy streams so numerous there. If you had approached a little closer you would have discovered that this dreadful creature had two legs and two arms, a head and a body, after all, in fact, that he was a *man*. Certainly his dress was rough and dirty, and he had with him some awkward-looking tools, and some queer sounds would proceed sometimes from his mouth; but if you took him as a whole, and stroked him the right way, for he really would let you come near him, you found him a very kind, genial, good-natured sort of fellow, very much like yourself in many ways. Yes, really, navvies are MEN; only they happened to get their long name from digging these trenches for inland navigation; and when canals were superseded by railways, the same class of men were employed, and the same name was applied to them in its abbreviated form. Probably their origin dates really much earlier than this; for, when I come to think, Egypt is a favourite abode of the alligator tribe, and no doubt whilst the alligators were swimming in the Nile thousands of years ago, the "human alligators," in the shape of Egyptian "navvies," were hewing out a fresh track for the Nile waters through some of the ancient Egyptian canals. Be this as it may, we have to deal with the navvy as he is. Pictures have been painted of him representing him as the "blackest of the black," a huge machine of flesh and blood, which only wants beef and beer to keep it going, especially the latter. "The roughest of the rough," "the most uncouth of the human species," "a roving pest to society," are among some of the terms in which I have heard him described. Whatever may have been the truth in the earlier days of navvying, these descriptions are not altogether true now. There are doubtless blackguards amongst the navvies, men who are a disgrace to their name and country, and almost to our common humanity; but to term the whole class a gang of unfeeling and unchristian reprobates is, to say the least of it, libellous. It is the camp-follower, the broken-down "cad," the scum of towns, who attach themselves to the navvy ranks, and bring with them very often a language more foul, and habits more disgusting, than they find there. They are not angels, by any means, but they are not all the coarse brutes they are represented to be. They are even spoken of sometimes as beings of a different race altogether. Who has not heard the story of the good woman who, when describing a railway accident to her neighbours, and summing up the result, related how there were three *men* killed, and a *navvy?* You see the poor woman had got into the habit of regarding them as though they were not of the same flesh and blood with herself.

Men! There are some of them whose hearts are as true, and whose lives are as upright, ay, and as pure, as those of some of their more highly favoured, and far more cultured brethren in better positions of life. Yes! infinitely more so. Don't let the fustian pea-jacket, the canvas trousers, the rainbow-coloured necktie, the smock-frock, or the hobnailed boots deceive you. Nor yet the horny hand nor the sunburnt and weather-beaten face. Of the navvy it is certainly very often true—

> "Within that rugged frame
> Burns a soul sincere."

When the first railway was started in Cornwall, and after the line was surveyed and preparations had been made for commencing, in due course the men appeared on the scene. It was mooted about the village of A—— that the first batch of navvies was likely to arrive on a certain evening, and the inhabitants were on the look-out for them. As soon as a party got in sight, the tidings quickly spread, and a boy rushed into the house of his mother, the wife of a small cottager, exclaiming, " Mother, the *navvies* have come!" The good housewife, not comprehending the nature of those new-comers, and wishing to be hospitable, is reported to have said in reply, "Eh! then run and open the stable door for 'em, and we'll give 'em a lodge."

C

This story was told me with great gusto by some of the men who worked there.

Another capital story is told to the same effect, of a woman who, meeting a navvy in a country lane, hastened to get out of his way, when our hero exclaimed, "You needn't be afeerd, ma'am, my mother was a *woman* !"

The author of "Little Rainbow" gives some amusing illustrations of the popular notion. She says in one of her accounts of the navvies, "In a village where many of them were lodged because a line was being made through part of it, some really Christian people declared that the navvies were 'too bad to be gone amongst, no good could be done.'"

A clergyman meeting a friend with some tracts in his hand, and hearing that they were to be distributed among the navvies, exclaimed, "Oh, won't they *rend* them ?"

I quite well remember when "I took to the line," and determined to accept the public call of my bishop and go and work amongst them, several of my friends entertained a lurking suspicion that I should soon return with a broken head, as they said in undertones, "They are desperate characters." Some even, judging from their language, feared I might get killed outright, I believe ; and most, that I should soon give up the task dispirited and sad at heart.

Dear navvies, some of you will read this—I write to you as you know I would if I were talking. Some of you are desperately bad characters, but I've known worse; you are not so bad as you are painted. You have managed to get a bad name, but you do not *all* deserve it. There is many a true man amongst you. Pull yourselves together a bit, lads, and show your better side, and let your defamers think the next time they meet any of you whether they have not made a mistake after all ; knock off a little of that extra beer, and just draw that language rather milder, and I venture to say that, even by these means, you will rub off a little of the dirt that somehow seems to cling to your names as well as to your boots. Forgive me, old friend, do you not think you could put a few shillings into the savings' bank for a rainy day? and if you could make up your mind "to stick to a job" a little bit longer at a time, it might be better for you, and the "gaffer" too. It is all very well, my boy, to speak of your "feet tickling for want of a walk," but a "jack-up" means a drink, and after the drink there's a long tramp very often; and a long tramp means no work, and no work means loss of self-respect, and if you once lose self-respect, you are "clean done." You are not a respectable navvy then at all, for a respectable navvy never likes to be wanting in self-respect, whatever else he may want.

Is that right now, or is it not? Your friend, the "Navvy Parson" ventures to think it is, and he hears some of you take up the phrase by which you generally give assent to a proposition, and say, "Right you are!" But I want to show some of your despisers that, though you have broad backs and sinewy muscles, and are often men of prodigious strength and endurance, you have often, nevertheless, hearts as tender and as kind as theirs. Some of you men who read this will remember a young Kentish navvy dying at Seaton huts. I do; I watched often by his bedside. When he died, a mate, who was a Kentish man, searched the line for Kent men to bear him to his last resting-place. So these sturdy, good-hearted lads gave up their day to carry their brother from his desolate chamber of death, and they each had a share in placing him in the earth, 'neath the shadow of the trees in the churchyard on the hill. There was a right feeling at work then.

You do not forget poor S——, who was killed by a fall down one of the shafts? How-nobly many of you fellows behaved. There was more than one bended knee which knelt around his dying form, as he lay gasping for breath at the hut door, whither you had borne him. There was more than one navvy's eye wet with tears of honest sympathy for the widow and her children. You were not long in getting that £80, or more, together to help them in their distress.

Whatever the navvies' faults and failings are, there is one splendid feature in their character. They are always ready and willing to help the sick, the suffering, and sorrowful, and that too with no niggard hand. It has even struck me, if I may address you again, that you are much too free often with what a Yorkshire navvy would call "the brass." When you meet a mate on tramp, or receive him within your hospitable door, give him, if you like, some "tommy" to help him on his way; but what is the use of making the poor fellow drunk ? Instead of getting on his way to the next stage in his march, he will find himself to-morrow morning waking up, after a sleep in a ditch, with aching limbs and a fevered frame. Yes ! There he goes ! You have "treated" him, as you call it. Look at him staggering along, hardly able to keep himself from overbalancing. What a figure he cuts, all through your mistaken kindness ! No wonder as the countryman meets him, he says to himself, "Here's another of these drunken navvies," and perhaps adds to his wife, if she is with him, "Mind yourself, or he'll roll up against you." You see that's how the bad name is got.

Lads ! Do they say you are all "regular rough ones " ? It is twelve o'clock at night. Look yonder, across the square in which the row of wooden houses stands. Do you see that light in "Darkey's" hut ? Do you know what is going on there ? Why, poor "Old Bricky-Ned" has had the misfortune to break his leg. Just peep

under the blind. There are Joe Baxter and Billy
Chump both sitting by his bedside, and nursing him
with all the tenderness, rough as it is, of a loving
woman, in spite of the fact too that they have both
been hard at work all day. Night after night, as
regularly as clock-work, you will find either Joe or Billy
at his bedside, ready to attend to his wants till he can
"do for himself a bit," and they do it expecting no re-
ward, often sacrificing a considerable part of their weekly
wages to minister to their sick brother's comforts and
necessities. Too often, however, there is a want of corre-
sponding gratitude on the part of the receiver of these
kindnesses. He frequently looks upon it as a matter of
course, as a navvy habit calling for no special recognition on his part; and after his recovery leaves the works,
as if he had received no kindness whatever.

But we may give another answer to the question,
"What is a navvy?" by picturing another scene. Just
look at the opposite side of the square. There is another
light burning. You need not go and take a peep there:
you can tell what is going on before you get near at all.
Such a row! "Rackety-Bob the Fiddler" lives there.
His hut is known as a regular drinking-shop. He has had
a party there "on the drink" all evening, and, of course,
they have ended up with a fight. The landlady has had
some of her best crockery smashed. "Surly-Bob" and
"Nailer" fall into the hands of the police, and are fined
for drunkenness. This gets into the penny local papers.
"Nobby" feels ashamed of a thrashing he got; "jacks
up," goes on tramp, passes through a score of villages
with a black eye, perhaps two, and of course people say,
"There is another of those navvies, look at his eyes;
they are always a-fighting!" Yes, that is just what they
say. Of course, it is not true, "always a-fighting!" But
you see how the bad name is got again. Let Master

" Rackety-Bob," in spite of his fiddling propensities, know that you are not the man for his hut. Pack up your " kit," and go to " Happy-Jim's," or one like his ; he and his good wife always keep things respectable there. If he gets a " rough one " who attempts to disturb the peace of his house, he very soon tells him that he must seek other quarters.

Mates ! the remedy is in your own hands. You need not have the bad name if you like to keep a good one.

The general answer to the question at the head of our chapter must be picked out from these and the following pages.

CHAPTER II.

NAVVY SLANG.

ANY attempt to write even a short account of the manners
and customs of the men who make our railways would
be very imperfect if it did not touch upon the extensive,
though decreasing, use of "slang" amongst them. A
residence only of a few days in their midst would be quite
sufficient to discover that our friends form no exception
to the general rule, that where large bodies of men are
congregated there will always be a multitude of slang
phrases, and many curious and often unique additions to
the vulgar tongue. The navvy and his fellow-workers
certainly yield their share. Indeed, there is scarcely a
class which has not its stock phrases and terms, from
Members of the British Parliament down to gipsies in a
tent. Sometimes they are witty, but they often approach
to irreverence. "Navvy" and "bricky" seem to them
amusing specimens of wit, clumsy and uncouth as they
are to a more educated mind. The bricklayers on a railway have a kind of cant or secret language which they
use more or less in common with the navvy; but it is
more frequently heard among the former than among the
latter.

These cant words and sayings seem to be made up of
terms very much like those in use amongst ordinary
mortals. A word or expression rhyming roughly with
the right word is often used. A sentence like the follow-

ing would be simply unintelligible to the uninitiated:—
"Now, Jack, I'm goin' to get a tiddley wink of pig's ear;
keep your mince pies on the Billy Gorman."

A tiddley wink of pig's ear!

Our first specimens will, I fear, shock the refined
ears of some readers. This strange combination is
mysterious; what does it mean? Simply this. It is an
instruction from a workman to his mate Jack, to keep
his eyes on the foreman or ganger, while he himself
goes to get a drink of beer. Had our friend wished
for something more potent than the pig's ear aforesaid,
he would have substituted the phrase, "Bryan o' lin,"
or, perhaps, "Tommy get out, and let your father in,"
meaning thereby *gin*.

The following conversation may often be heard:—

"Well, old man, I see you've jacked up; what's your
little game now?"

"Oh! I'm goin' to get my 'kit' (bundle), and be off
on the frog and toad."

The motion of the two reptiles is suggestive, as I
suppose, of a man on tramp. Before starting, however,
if he were at all inclined to be a dandy, he would express
his determination, which he would carry out at the hut
door, "to blackbird and thrush round his daisy roots."

This is still more mysterious. Not so, when we consider that one of these birds of song represents "blacking,"
and the other the "brush;" and the hobnailed boots, which
are to undergo the process of cleaning, are by an extraordi-
nary poetical license termed his "daisy roots." Whether,
because the impression of them on the gentle flower
would leave nothing but the root remaining, I cannot
say. If he had spoken in plain English, he would have
said, "I shall pack up my bundle, clean my boots, and
be off on tramp."

A new-comer to the works is sometimes thus addressed

by a ganger given to use slang, and the terms are more puzzling, and perhaps more silly than ever :—

"Now, then, my china-plate, out with your cherry-ripe, off with your steam-packet, and set your bark and growl agoin'."

This is essentially a bricklayer's phrase.

If for "china-plate" you substitute "mate," and put "pipe" for "cherry-ripe," "jacket" for "steam-packet," and for "bark and growl" read "trowel," the puzzle is revealed.

One morning I heard a man say he had made a fool of himself the night before, because he "had been and got the elephant's trunk;" and as Edmond's Menagerie had actually been exhibiting in the next town on the previous evening, in my innocence I thought possibly he had been playing some trick with one of the elephants in the collection. So I inquired, and the man seemed somewhat abashed and awkward about it. On pressing my question, I discovered that "getting the elephant's trunk," meant nothing more or less than this, that he had been drunk ; alluding no doubt to the capacity of the trunk of one of those animals in taking up supplies of liquid. This was a phrase I afterwards frequently heard. A bricklayer often says to his comrade at the work, "Lend us your panorama,"—this being merely a picturesque request for the loan of his hammer.

If he runs short of bricks, he cries out to his "cad" (assistant) for "Dublin tricks," and if he wants water, he makes a demand for "the fisherman's daughter."

When a man gets tired of walking a long distance to his work, supposing he can get no lodgings nearer, if he wishes to express himself in the approved slang phraseology, he will do it thus :—

"I can't stand this Duke of York to my Russian-Turk;

I shall go and get my sugar and honey and be off to another Solomon."

A strange medley this, which requires some patience both to listen to as well as to unravel. It will read all right when we have applied the substitution process.

The distinguished peer means "walk." The Russian-Turk is a long way of saying the very short word "work." Instead of sugar and honey you must read "money," and put "job" for Solomon. Then here is the translation, "I cannot 'stand' this long walk to my work; I shall go and get my money and go to another job."

The straps which a navvy wears round his legs are usually called "London and Yorks." He generally wears these when on tramp. The great road of communication from North to South in old days was the road from London to York, known as the Great North road, and navvies often selected this as their route; and I suppose now you would meet more "tramps" on that and the Watling Street road than any other.

I suppose Russian and Turk contain an allusion to the struggle between the two countries, signifying hard, tough work. "Sugar and honey" is merely a stupid rhyme; as for "Solomon" and "job," it will take a wiser man than myself to solve the relation of the terms.

Supposing our wearied workman to be on his way to fresh scenes of labour, a new man must be sought to fill his place. When applied to by the "ganger," he would announce his willingness to "make a puff and dart" (start) in the morning. A common custom on the line, if a man wishes to know the time, is to inquire, "What's the bird lime?"

"Johnny Randle," stands for a "candle," whilst a shovel is dignified by the name of "Lord Lovel," and is generally spoken of as "the Navvy's Prayer-Book."

I have been told, though I have never heard the
expression myself, that often when a man is ready to
retire to rest, he will inform his mates, "That he's done his
lot for the day, and is goin' to lay his pen'oth o' bread (head)
on the weeping-willow (pillow), and do a little bo-peep"
(sleep). It is very strange how the prefix "Charley"
has become attached to many sayings of theirs, for
instance, "Charley Randy" for brandy, "Charley Frisky"
for whisky. "Charley Prescot" is simply another name
for a waistcoat. "Jimmy Skinner" stands for dinner.

Inspectors are not always welcome visitors to a man
when he feels "a bit gammy" (idle); accordingly a request
is sometimes addressed to a mate in the following terms:
—"Nobby, I'm going to do a 'laugh and joke,' let me
know if you 'twig the spider.'" He intends, that is, to
smoke, and wishes to avoid being caught by the inspector.
If Nobby happens to be inclined to do his friend a good
turn, he will inform him of the approach of the said
authority in the words, "Look out, here comes heap of
coke."

The earth which is carried away in waggons is distinguished by the name of "crock," or more commonly
"muck." Navvies themselves speak of one another as
"muck-shifters," or "thick-legs."

There are, no doubt, hundreds of other and such-like
phrases in common use; I have recorded these few as
specimens. The men also frequently apply slang phrases
to the different gangs at work, according to the place in
which they lodge, or from circumstances connected with
them as a body. For instance, on a certain railway line
a large number lodged in an inn having the sign of
"The Horse Shoes," and from this there came two sets,
one known as "The Horse-shoe Gang," the other as
the "Horse-shoe Shoe-blacks." Then one has heard of
"The Old Ninety-Fifth," a celebrated gang in the earlier

days of navvying. There are very few members of this left now. A new lot of men is often spoken of as "The Boys' Gang," while those who do their work quickly are known as "Fly-away Gangs."

The clergy are playfully spoken of as "The Billycock Gang," but from my experience, I must say that the navvy is always very respectful to members of this gang, and is always ready to touch his wide-awake as they pass.

CHAPTER III.

NICKNAMES.

CLOSELY allied to the subject of slang, common among
navvies and their associates, is that of nicknames, of
which there is a vast number. A most interesting
field of inquiry is opened out here. Nicknames and
aliases abound, enough to fill a whole volume. Let us
speak of the "aliases" first. Generally, the adoption of
the "alias" is considered an unsatisfactory proceeding;
but it must not be supposed because our "navvy" friend
is known by one name in one place, and a different name
in another, he is on that account a shady character.
On one line he may have the name of "Stumps," and
on a second that of "Tramping-Tom," and yet have
committed no special wrong which would lead him to
hide his real name. A man may get a new name on
almost every "job" to which he goes, if he doesn't know
any of the workmen there, or the same name may stick
to him for years. As a rule, I confess it *looks* suspicious,
and *is* very often more, when the name of a *family* is
being constantly changed. If a man moves off with
his wife and family by moonlight, all in a hurry, as they
say, you probably would not find the same name on his
door-plate, if he had one, at his next halting-place as
at his last. The neighbouring tradesmen might inquire
in vain for the customer whose name stood in their
ledger as Q——. Most of our navvies, however, are not

ashamed of their own names, though necessity, wit, carelessness, and many other circumstances, often brand them with names very unlike their own. Time-keepers do not understand the subtleties of Smith *minor* and Smith *major*, as we say at school. Sometimes in a deep cutting, where a hundred men or more are at work, there are several of the same name; some distinguishing epithet is then applied to them either by the time-keeper, the ganger, or the men themselves, and this often sticks to them through life.

A time-keeper told me this story of two men who came to him one day when he had a large gang at work. The two were known to be rather rough characters, and on their names being asked, they at once gave those of the contractors, "Oh, put me down '*Lucas*,' and him '*Aird*.'" The time-keeper, not wishing his chiefs to have their names associated with two known shady characters, much to his credit, at once refused, and two others were selected as being more appropriate.

Mrs. Garnett, in her "Plea for the Navvy," tells a striking story illustrative of the custom of the acquisition of aliases.

"A handsome young man, an only son, was killed thirty years ago at a public work, to which immediately afterwards came a young engine-man and his wife. The new-comer was remarkably like the dead young man. The navvies said, 'Why, here is a new —— come to take his place.' Ever since, not only the engine-man, but his wife and children, have been called by that young man's name."

If this book should fall into the hands of any of my old friends or others who have adopted an alias, let me remind them that the adoption might prove very awkward for them in case of money being left to them. Even in the matter of post-office savings' bank deposits, had I chosen, in several instances I might have put some depositors to serious inconvenience by disclosing their real names. Though I was perfectly satisfied that the deposit was placed there by the person named in the book, yet I knew in confidence that the name so entered was not his own. It sometimes happens that a young lad leaves his native village, leads a roving life for several years, and at length comes back again a grown man, and works on a new line in the neighbourhood of his birth with an entirely new name ; and if he chooses to conceal his identity, he is even unknown by his friends and relations, who have given him up as lost for many a year.

We have to speak now of the kindred subject of nicknames. They very seldom give offence, and though the custom is not so extensive as it used to be, it is sufficiently in vogue to form a striking feature in navvy lore. Considerably more than half the men, from the chief agent to the most insignificant "nipper at the points," have some amusing title, which is given for reasons connected in some way with incidents of their life, their character, manners, conversation, appearance, place of birth. It would be next to impossible to classify all the various groups of nicknames, though many admit of classification. What the Smiths, the Joneses, the Browns, and the Robinsons, for instance, are to the whole tribe of Englishmen, so are the " Punches," the " Gingers," the " Nobbies," the " Slens," and the " Codgers " to the race of navvies. Let us have a look at a few of them. Friend " Punch " is to open the ball. Now we must not suppose " Punch " necessarily receives his title from his love of the flowing bowl, as he *may* be a rigid teetotaller, nor yet from the necessary possession of any peculiarly comic character which may seem to connect him with the periodical of the name. No ! If a man does not attain to a stature of average height, in fact, if he is short and stumpy, and goes on tramp to a railroad, he may expect any hour to be dubbed " Punch." If he betrays any additional peculiarity he will soon get a prefix to that. If his breadth correspond somewhat nearly to his height, it might be at once " Ten-ton Punch," or if he should happen to come on to the works with his hair rather long at the back, he might expect to be " Pig-tail Punch." If very short and thin, he would be knighted "Fanny Punch." Occasionally, for the sake of distinction, Mr. Punch gets his additional title from the ganger in whose set he works, for instance,—pardon me if you read it, friend John,—" Jack Brett's Punch." But there are other variations : "Tin Whistle," "Sore-eyed," "Chattering," and "Tea-pot" Punches speak for themselves. Not so "Dolly-legged Punch,"—thereby hangs a tale, yes, a new version of "The Tale of a Tub." Now you must know that washing in many of the huts, as in more civilised regions, is done in what is called a dolly-tub, in the bottom of which the clothes are twirled about by a three-legged instrument called a " dolly." The Punch in question objected to his landlady washing his belongings with this article, as he asserted, what many careful housewives would bear out, that it wore out the clothes. So one night he quietly took a saw and deprived "dolly" of its objectionable appendages. However, he was discovered, and is constantly reminded of the episode by the quaint *sobriquet* which has ever since clung to him.

Now, let us go from short and stout to tall and thin. I knew of two brothers, both above the ordinary height, who rejoiced in the titles of "Shadow" and "Bones." There are many other names which apply for the same reason, to wit, "Kangaroo," "Slenderman," more frequently abbreviated to "Slen," "Straight-up Gip," and "Starch-'em-Stiff." Should length of nose be as promi-

nent a feature as length of legs and body, " Tweedle-Beak "
and " Snipe-Nose " will soon be applied, or even more
commonly " Duke," out of compliment to the Great
Duke.

It is rather hard on the maimed that their misfor-
tunes should brand them with a name which must often
wound them deeply. While all the minor improprieties
and peculiarities of temperament, character, and appearance are fair objects of ridicule and joke, I should like
to see this custom dropped wherever a reference to
bodily ailments and imperfections must give pain. If a
poor fellow has the misfortune to lose an eye, he gains
the name of " Gunner;" if he is short of a leg or an arm,
" Peggy " or " Wingy " is at once affixed to him; or if the
arms a man may be fortunate enough to possess are
rather longer than usual and quick in motion, he is
" Bees'-Wings ; " or if one eye rather overlooks the other,
he is " Boss " directly. Even " Wingy " and " Peggy "
have variations. I have come across the name " Rainbow-
Peg." What the connection between a wooden leg and
a rainbow was I could not imagine ; unless, as I thought,
the unfortunate possessor had painted his stump of
various hues. Not so, however ; Rainbow's wooden leg
had become by degrees very much worn, and as the
nature of the work which was allotted to him caused him
to stand about for a long time, he threw much of his
weight on to his sound limb, which, being naturally
somewhat bowed, had in time, from extra pressure,
approached a semicircle, and hence the name. To this
class may be added " Web-footed-Sall," the " Boss-eyed
Cheshireman," and " Crutchy-Dick," and the oft-repeated
" Chump " in endless variety. A man's whiskers come
in for a share of the fun, as " Streaky-Dick," " Ginger-
Bill," and " Black-and-Tan " could tell you. A man with
red hair would be termed a " Copper-knob," or " Maho-

D

gany top." Perhaps the most common source of these curious additions to the register roll is the place of a man's birth. Of these " Bristol Jack," " Oxford Joe," " Brummagem Bob," " Yankee Tom," " Devon Bill," " Yorkey," and " Gloster " are samples, and they are as numerous as the names of all the counties in the United Kingdom. All Lancashire men get the shortened title of " Lank," with numerous prefixes, *e.g.*, " Tailboard-Lank," " Bacca-Lank."

But there was one " Yorkey " whose strange history calls for special mention. He is dead and gone, poor fellow! but his oddities survive him. He was a well-known character on railroads for many years. " Contrairy-York " was the name with which he was most familiar: he seems to have gained it from the fact of his eccentric obstinacy. The landlady of any hut where he lodged would be ready with a volume of queer stories respecting him. One morning, for instance, bread and milk was the general order for breakfast. Everybody had his portion boiled, except " Contrairy," who insisted it must be *fried*, as he called it.

Another day he is on tramp with two or three of his mates ; they approach a stream of considerable breadth, his fellow-travellers cross by the bridge, which spans the stream close by. Not so " Yorkey "—was not his name " Contrairy " ?—true to it, he walks through the water. And now look at the party going up the hill beyond, it will not take you long to single out the hero of the company, even were his clothes not dripping with water from the stream. Look at his legs, one trouser leg rolled up nearly to the knee displaying a blue stocking, the other within two inches of the top of his boots, exhibiting white hose. Peeping over his shoulder is the cat which he usually carries about with him, because most other navvies, if they have a pet, prefer the dog. Many a queer yarn of this Yorkey's odd whims have I heard spun.

Why a Welshman should be termed a "Mountain-pecker," and a Wiltshireman a "Moon-raker," I must leave my readers to guess; and I should be greatly obliged if they would unravel the mystery of "Skee-dicks," "Acamaraclous," and "Okem-finney-Joe," or tell me why an old-fashioned youth generally gets styled "Gezer." I wonder whether "Joey-on-the-Crank" could give any prison experience. I am sure my old friends, "Concertina-Cockney" and "Jew's-harp-Jack" could play a merry tune on the instruments with which their names are connected. "Jimmy-the-new-man," and "Johnny-come-lately," evidently did not arrive on the works where they first got their name until some time after their commencement. They must both have a place on our list, and so must he who happened one day to look down one of the pits after a blasting operation, and observing a cloud of smoke rising in volumes, exclaimed with true Yorkshire accent, "What a reeky hoile!" This was quite enough for the bystanders on which to exercise their wit, and from that time our friend was known, if you please, as "Reeky-Hoile."

I said in the earlier part of this chapter that the family of "Nobbies" was a numerous one. It ranges from plain "Nobby," to the more expressive titles of "Sump-hole Nobby," and "Scented-soap Nobby." Such names as these, too, are not uncommon, "Beer," "Brandy," "Fatbuck," "Hopper," "Scandalous," "Chinaman," and "Rainbow-ratty." To return to the more out-of-the-way titles, I have never been able to discover why a once well-known character on railway works, now dead, received the name of "Tommy the Gate." Poor Tommy is the subject of many a long yarn. Tommy was a Welshman. He first saw the light, he said, in one of Pickford's waggons; when he arrived at the age of manhood, he tried his hand at pig dealing, and this failing, he took to a roving navvy life, becoming a sort of " hanger on," at the various hut settlements of the land.   I am told he never slept on a bed for twenty years, always preferring a hard board; and when at last he was no longer able to tramp about from place to place, and was taken to a workhouse and made to sleep in a bed, he declared that the change would kill him, and as the story goes, he died very soon afterwards.

Another remarkable character was " Gentleman Sydney," but I have not been able to get reliable details as to his history.   Navvies are by no means indifferent to the charms of nature.   There goes one with a bright flower and "a bit o' green stuff" in his button-hole, that's " Primrose Bob;" and there, too, walking towards the porch of the Mission Church is " Violet Tom," with a neat little bunch of the gentle flower adorning his Sunday coat.   Any of these little things gives rise to a name which sticks to the possessor of it till the violets and primroses shed their fragrance over his grave.

CHAPTER IV.

HUT LIFE.

THERE are many picturesque lights and shades in connection with the life of a navvy, perhaps none so quaintly
striking as his usual place of abode. A description of a
settler's home in his log-built house in Canadian backwoods, or the bushranger's shelter on Australian sheep-
walks would, in some respects, correspond with an
account of the railroad hut. We have already taken a
peep at the little colonies as they crown the hills, cluster
down the slopes of the undulating ground, or nestle in
the valleys and woods half hidden by the trees. But we
must give a more detailed description. One was quite
sorry to see them disappear, for they added a colonial
picturesqueness to the districts where they stood, and
the places they once occupied now look desolate and for-
saken. Navvies' huts are constructed in various ways.
The simplest is that of the "nipper at the points," who
artfully burrows a cavern out of the side of the clay
bank, and collects stray bits of wood and felt, and arches
over the entrance with the rough awning of a ragged piece
of tarpaulin, which he weights with "brickbats;" and
here from morn till night he shelters himself from the
winter's blast or summer's sun, popping to and fro to
his work like a rabbit playing gambols in a warren.
The next stage of hut is the miner's cabin. At every pit-
head is a roughly-constructed shelter of wood, more or

less draughty, sometimes consisting of a few slabs of
timber fastened together and covered with large pieces
of felting and such like. These serve as a refuge at
night when the men ascend to supper, or wait their turn
to go below. Many a yarn has been spun in these
during the long winter evenings, as the beacon light
blazed in at the open door, and the fire on the rude
hearth crackled in harmony with the scene around.
It was a curious sight to walk up the line at nine or ten
o'clock, or even later, and look in at the groups of workmen as they clustered round the fire. And there was much
to be learnt from a quiet chat with them, as they sat,
some on the floor, some on rude benches supported by
piles of bricks, or on an upturned hod, or heaps of picks
and spades. What queer little nooks some of the next
class were! As you looked at them you might have
imagined yourself in the wild regions of the Emerald
Isle. They only wanted the hills of Connemara in the
background, and Paddy and his pig at the door to make
the scene complete. Indeed, the pig was often there,
and sometimes "Paddy," too. The four walls were built
of turf, large square sods of earth piled one on the other
till they reached the height of five or six feet. These
supported a low depressed roof of timber covered with
the usual felting. The interior consisted of three compartments divided off by partitions of boards. I knew
of one such hut as this having been ingeniously converted into a two-storied mansion, not by the usual
process, however, of raising the roof. The occupants
erected a sort of huge wooden "meat-safe," depending
from the rafters and steadied by the tie beam. This was
reached by a movable ladder, and when I came to ask
of its use, I was informed, "Oh, that be where the brats
sleep." A sort of "brat-cage," in fact. Out of justice
to the contractors, I must say this was a solitary case,

and was unknown to them, or, doubtless, such an arrangement would not have been allowed. These turf huts
are amongst the most picturesque, and *look* very snug in
their way; but they are dusty, stuffy, and dirty to a
very dangerous extent. Let the landlady be as cleanly
as she will, she can't keep them decent. In such huts
as these it is not an uncommon sight to see fungi growing on the wall, and in winter even an icicle occasionally hanging down from the ridge tree. It is next to
impossible to keep the damp from penetrating on every
side. For the sake of the health of the men and their
families, and, indeed, in the interest of the employer, the
sooner they are disused the better. The doctors will
bear me out in saying that the great majority of cases of
ordinary sickness are to be found existing in the huts of
this class, for they are a violation of many of the ordinary sanitary conditions. Happily, in the Kettering and
Manton Railway they were not numerous, but sufficiently
so to give the writer a very decided opinion as to their
inconvenience—I might say unfitness—for human habi-
tation. I have, not long since, walked over the ground
where some of them stood, and looked at the walls of the
now tenantless homes. That I may never again see men,
women, and children huddling and crowding together as
I have in some of these tenements, is one of my most
fervent wishes!

Just as all navvies are not the mere cattle and swine
they are often supposed and represented to be, so all huts
are not mere wattle and daub, in which one would hardly
like to keep a cow. Some are much better than others;
in fact, the majority of huts were of the class I am now
going to describe. These were built almost entirely of
wood. Wooden walls, sometimes with a coating of gas-
tar, occasionally of whitewash, wooden roofs covered
with black felt, with a low, squat, red-brick chimney,

three windows, and a door back and front, constitute their
external appearance. A common hut of this type, as
nearly all others, is divided into three parts. The central
hall is the common living room of the whole family,
father, mother, children, and lodgers. This room has the
back and front doors alluded to, with occasionally, though
not often, a porch over one or both these doors. To my
mind this arrangement is very decidedly favourable to the
sanitary condition of the huts, if not to the landlady's
temper, as very often a current of air sweeps through.
To the right and left of this central hall are the bedrooms,
one for the landlord and his wife and children, the other
for the lodgers. Walk in! How busy the scene! A
bright fire is blazing. The landlady is eagerly intent,
with her sleeves rolled up, making preparations for the
hungry party about to come in. The elder children, just
home from the Mission school, are "laying out the table,"
and assisting in other necessary household work. Look
round you! There are two tables, one on either side
of the room. In one corner are shelves with rows of
glasses and other tokens of the thirsty nature of these
sons of toil, a few books well-thumbed by many a reader,
a cruet-stand which has seen better days, a blacking
brush or two, and half a dozen empty spirit bottles.
There is another shelf behind you, running all across the
room, occupied likewise with a very miscellaneous selec-
tion of household ware, strangely intermingled with
ornaments of all shapes and sizes. The walls themselves are often to be seen very neatly covered with
pretty papers bought in the neighbouring town ; but not
so pleasing are the pictures of "horrors" from cuttings
of the latest "Police News" and other "Penny Dread-
fuls." The highly-finished photograph, and the elaborately
painted portrait from the Tradesman's Almanack, funeral
cards deeply embosomed in black, with verses to match,

and weeping willows with angels crouching beneath them
in tearful attitude, gaily coloured copies of the "Flight
into Egypt," and such like are commonly seen adorning
the walls. Don't be surprised if you should see the
room covered with patchwork squares from a paper-
hanger's pattern-book. Perhaps of all pictures the
most acceptable, and after our first year's mission work,
most frequently to be seen, were the well-known cartoons
of the "British Workman" and the "Gospeller." These
were eagerly sought after, and soon the coarse figures of
the "Police News" got their faces daubed with the paste
brush, and disappeared behind pictures of a better class.
Mind your head! or you will bring it in contact with
some of the numerous fly cages, boots, or other articles
which hang from the cross-beams; or if it is Christmas
time, look up at that gaily dressed branch of fir suspended from the roof-tree, with its ornaments glittering
in the firelight. You need not be afraid of treading on
the carpet, for it is of a material which stands hard wear
and of a pattern which does not quickly fade. It is of
brick, and if the landlady is a tidy woman you will soon
find an electric sensation running through your feet from
the crunching of the silver sand with which she has
strewn the floor. Whilst we have been looking round,
the lodgers have arrived. There's "Slurry-Cart Jack,"
with his shirt-sleeves tucked up, washing his hands in
the tub at the back door, while "Snipey" is drying his
on a roller inside the said door. There is "Happy-Joe"
already with "Little Curly," a child of two years, on
one knee, pulling his nose, and "Nell," with one arm
round his neck, while he is attempting to put an orange
slyly into the pocket of her dress. "Happy-Joe" always
makes much of the little ones, and they will often trot
out over the green to meet him. "Mousey-Dick" has
to be back early at his work, a special "job" which he

has undertaken at his own risk, so he sits down at once
to his dinner. Soon round the table, on forms, are
ranged a band of hungry men, with their pots of ale and
plates of meat, and steaming piles of potatoes, "going at
it" in right earnest. So we will leave them and see
where that door on the right leads to, for our friends,
like other folks, do not care for prying eyes at meal
times. This is the lodgers' bedroom. There is not
much to see here. Five wooden bedsteads, all very close
together, with room for two in a bed, made often of a
mattress stuffed with straw, covered with brown or light-
blue coverlets, a few boxes standing in one corner, a
"kit" or two hanging from the beams, comprise the
furniture of this apartment. We will ask to be allowed
to see the room at the other end of the hut. Papered
with bright patterns or sheets of newspaper, it looks
clean and tidy. The bedsteads here are of iron and the
coverlets white, and altogether an air of superior comfort
surrounds you. There is the curtain dividing the room
into two compartments, if there are children, though
often such a division is wanting. A chest of drawers
covered with a white towel and surmounted by a looking-
glass; and boxes piled one on the other, crowned with a
and basin, complete this scene. No, not quite. I ought
not to have forgotten the inevitable beer barrel, and
sometimes two or three. This bedroom is invariably the
cellar of the establishment, which is always presided over
by the landlady, who pays many visits to this shrine
daily to fill the foaming jugs for her too numerous
applicants.

The wooden hut is occasionally varied by erections
of brick, but the interior and domestic arrangements
are the same. The better class of wooden and brick
huts are furnished often with much taste, and sometimes
even with elegance, the floors being carpeted and the

rooms fitted with as much comfort as is to be found in the houses of better class artisans; while in some few, not many, you might almost suppose you had found your way into an officer's quarters in camp. Handsome clocks, cases of stuffed birds and animals, small articles of *vertu*, sewing machines, musical instruments are to be found in huts of this description, though I have not yet heard of a pianoforte there; we leave that to the merry miners of the North. They are not only very comfortable some of these dwellings, but they occasionally have " fashionable " names attached to them, for instance there was " The West End " at Glaston, and " The Terrace," too. Who does not remember at Seaton " The Hermitage " and its pretty curtains, and " Rose Cottage," the sweet flowers in the garden, with a little fountain playing in the midst ?

All this serves to show that there is not that utter and universal want of taste and civilisation among our railway makers which is generally supposed.

Look yonder ! There go eight lodgers to the hut across the square. Now, my good woman, you must move about sharply, or you will not be able to keep them in good temper; they are very hungry, and you told me the other day that they all boarded themselves, and that you had to cook separate dinners for each of the eight; and several of them had an entirely different sort of dish. Cooking in a hut is no light work. You do wisely, good mother, in summer, to keep your caldron boiling on the fire you have, gipsy-like, made outside your hut door, so that you may keep the place cool. For huts, be it remembered, are *very* cold in winter, and equally scorching in the hot weather.

Now I want to have a word with the wives and daughters in the huts. Some of you will have this book on your shelf, and will read this chapter with the others.

As your cooking is over after one o'clock on Sunday, do
you not think you could spare one hour or so on Sunday
evening? Your little Mission church is not far off, and
you know you will be right welcome. What a change it
would be from the hurry and scurry of your every-day
life! and you would discover, too, that you would get
through things in the week with a lighter heart.
And, above all, you should not forget Him to
whom you owe so much; you would then be preparing
yourself for a better place after your life of change and
unrest is over. Navvy children are generally to be
found at the church, why should there not be more
mothers and elder sisters there?

For you, too, landlord, I have a word. Can't you
move off those fellows just outside your back window?
You know they will only get you into trouble. There
are six of them playing at "pitch and toss." Now, stop
it, and remind them it's Sunday morning, and set them
a good example by going to a place of worship. The
lodgers will be much influenced by your mode of spending Sunday. If you make your hut a public-house, as
too many of you do, what then can you expect but a
scene of drunken uproar? A quiet hut and a happy
Sunday depends, landlords, on yourselves. Look to it,
and see that you have both. Why should a few rowdy,
besotted reprobates and the ill-gotten gains from the
drunkard's pence deprive you of what ought to be one
of the working man's choicest treasures, a quiet, peaceful,
and holy Sunday, free from work, and dedicated to the
refreshment of soul and body, and, above all, to God?

In this account of hut life, it may be inquired how the
men fill up their spare time. In a hundred different
ways, of which I am afraid one of the most common is to
sit on a form with two elbows on the table, talk, sip pots of
beer, unlimited in quantity, and too often very indifferent

in quality. You may go into huts any evening, and see poor unfortunate wretches whom drink has dragged to the lowest depths of misery, in all stages of intoxication, some fuddled and stupid, some talkative and foolish, some noisy and rough, and others thoroughly overcome, and on their backs. In short, the huts are, alas! too commonly converted into unlicensed public-houses.

Landlady, I say, look at poor Jack; you have sold him a quart more already than he ought to have had. Will you, eager for his pence, run off again to the beer barrel in the bedroom and fetch him another "tot"? Not if you are a true woman; if you desire to keep a peaceful home and a quiet conscience, you will say, "Jack, you have had enough, and not a drop more will you get in my hut to-night." Don't be afraid, foolish Jack will respect you all the more for it to-morrow, when his senses have come back to him. Of course he will threaten to leave you and go to "Ned Soaker's," but he won't go if you speak kindly and nicely to him, as you know how. Even if he does go, you will get a better man perhaps in his place, for it will soon become known on the works that " Brighton George's " wife keeps a "quiet shop."

When the evening draws in, it is not an unusual sight to see a group of men at one corner of the hut table playing at cards, in another quarter of the room shove halfpenny is the game, whilst near the chimney is an acquaintance, "Schemer," carving little wooden toys for the children; another is writing a letter, or perhaps reading one of the books from the Mission library. Or, you may enter another hut and look on quite a different scene: there is a group round the fire all listening attentively to a mate as he reads an article from one of the weekly papers, or an account of some interesting event known and talked of amongst the men. Could

you have gone the round of the huts at the time of the
colliery accident in Wales, when a number of men were
imprisoned in a living tomb, night after night you would
have heard the story read with increasing interest. Anything touching railroad life, too, is always eagerly listened
to.

In the summer time quoits and cricket are among the
favourite pastimes.   These are varied by an occasional
dog race ; and one sometimes sees a lively game of leap-
frog among the more frolicsome.   The poultry, the pig,
and occasionally a little bit of garden, demand attention.
Railway people are very fond of pets ; nearly always
there is a dog, sometimes two or three in each hut, and I
have seen even pet lambs, pigeons, and tame rabbits.
Birds of all kinds abound, and once I saw a pet
monkey.   The weakness for keeping lurcher dogs occasionally got the men into trouble with the neighbouring
keepers ; but the navvies have too often been made a
scape-goat for other people's offences in this matter.

At one hut settlement there was a resident poetess ;
her inspirations were printed and circulated in the huts,
but I have not heard of any one having had time to read
them.

If hut life has its inconveniences and discomforts, it
has, too, its romantic and attractive side, which serves to
soften its many hardships and to render it pleasant rather
than otherwise to those who have adopted a roving
profession.   There remains yet another class of hut, of
which the next chapter shall speak.

CHAPTER V.

SHANTIES AND SHELTERS.

ANYBODY who knows anything about "navvies," knows something of the "shanty" system. It is one of the most striking, at the same time one of the most painful, and, I fear I must add, one of the necessary features of navvy life. Its debasing, demoralising influences in times past, and even now, are too apparent. Yet, conducted on true lines, it may be made a powerful influence both for the comfort, the instruction, and even general elevation of the men. As it ordinarily exists, I have no hesitation in condemning it as a social misfortune to the navvy to be obliged to submit to it. As it might exist, and would exist, if contractors would follow a few noble examples, it would, to say the least of it, be an exceedingly different affair altogether. I should like to contrast the state of things connected with the shanty system of fifty years ago and that of the present day, and ask, whether, as a rule, there has been any improvement commensurate with the advance of the time. For the picture of shanty life in the early days of the railway, I refer my readers to a striking account given in "Household Words" some years since. I do not know the author's name, but he was a man who had been well educated, and evidently got on well in the world, but for some time he worked as a navvy and had personal experience of their habits. The writer relates, how, in the

year 1834, he completed his education at a school near
Harrow, how he climbed the playground wall to watch
railway works in progress near, and how he was seized
with a strong desire to be an engineer.   He tells how
he bought books on the subject, how his guardian opposed
his wish, and that early one morning in March 1835,
with a bundle on his arm and a few shillings in his
pocket, he ran away from home and walked to the
nearest railway works.   Arriving there, after a tramp of
thirty miles, he obtained work as a tip-driver, but one
day having succeeded in driving horse and truck together
over the tip-head, he was reprimanded, and he set off
again, and obtained work as a bucket-steerer in one of
the shafts of Watford tunnel.   In due course he was
shifted to a gang of regular navvies in the tunnel.   He
says, " This gang consisted of some forty men, each of
whom bore a nickname.   There were ' Happy - Jack,'
' Long-Bob,'   ' Dusty-Tom,'   ' Billygoat,'   ' Frying-Pan,'
' Red-Head.'   For myself, my new clothes and tools
entitled me to the style of ' Dandy-Dick.' "   He was
fined two gallons " footing," was put to work with a lad
called " Kick-Daddy ; " in cleaning out a trench he made
a chum of a man called " Canting George," and his ganger
rejoiced in the title of " Bullhead."

Our friend " Dandy-Dick," for so we will call him, continuing his narrative, writes a very graphic account of a
shanty or tommy shop as it existed in those days, not by
any means unlike those existing now.

" The shanty was a building of stone, brick, mud,
timber, and partly roofed with tile and partly with
tarpaulin.   It consisted of a single oblong room, and
stood upon a piece of ground near the tunnel mouth.
Almost every gang of navvies, and there were sixty at
least employed on the tunnel, was thus lodged, so that

there were several of these dens of wild men round
about the works.

" The domestic arrangements of the navigators' shanties
were presided over by a set of blear-eyed old crones, of
whom there was one to each gang. They were expected
to cook, to make the beds, wash and mend the clothes of
their masters, who beat them fearfully whenever the
fancy of one or more of these rough lords and masters
inclined to that refreshment. In all the obscenity and
blasphemy they bore their part, in the fighting they also
lent a hand. With features frightfully disfigured, with
heads cut and bandaged, they made themselves at home
in the midst of everything from which pride and virtue
shrink aghast.

" Once only I visited a shanty. I was in spare hours
teaching George Hatley to read : and it happened one
Sunday morning, early in May, that the rain hindering
church attendance, I strolled up to the shanty to find
George ; but he was gone out. Old Peg, the presiding
crone, who was then exhibiting two black eyes and a
bandaged chin, told me he would be back by eleven. It
was then past ten, and having cursed me in a way
intended to be very friendly, she invited me to wait till
he returned. So I sat down on a three-legged stool and
took a survey of the place.

" The door was open about midway in one of the sides,
having a window on each side of it, and near one of the
windows were a few rude benches and seats. Of such of
my comrades as were up, four or five were sprawling on
these seats, two lying flat on the earthen floor playing at
cards, and one sat on a stool mending his boots. These
men all greeted me with a gruff welcome, and pressed
me to drink. Near the other window were three. barrels
of beer, all in tap, the keys of which were chained to a
stout leather girdle which encircled old Peg's waist.

E

Her seat, an old-fashioned arm-chair, was handy to these barrels, of which she was tapster. The opposite side and one end of the building were fitted up from floor to roof, which was low, in a manner similar to the between-decks of an emigrant ship. In each of the berths lay one or two of my mates, for this was their knock-off Sunday; all drunk or asleep, each man lay with his head on his kit; and nestling with many of the men, were dogs and litters of puppies of the bull or lurcher breed, for a navvy's dog was of course either for fighting or poaching.

" The other end of the room served as a kitchen. There was a rude dresser in one corner, and a rickety table, on which was arranged a very miscellaneous set of plates and dishes, in tin, wood, earthenware, each holding an equally ill-matched cup, basin, or bowl. Against the wall was fixed a double row of cupboards or lockers, one to each man, these were the tommy boxes ; below them, suspended from stout nails and hooks, were several large pots and pans. Over the fireplace, which was nearly central, hung about a dozen guns. In the other corner was a large copper, beneath which a blazing fire was roaring, a volume of savoury steam escaping beneath the lid, and old Peg, muttering and spluttering, ever and anon threw on more coals and kept the copper boiling. Now, as I looked at this copper, I noticed a riddle, not particularly hard to solve. Depending over it were several strings, communicating with the interior, and to each of these was attached a piece of wood. Peg, muttering and spluttering, traced one or more of these mysteries. I asked her the meaning of them.

" ' Them !' said Peg, speaking in a broad Lancashire dialect, and taking a stick in her hand, ' why, sith'ee lad, this bit o' stick has four nicks on't, well it's Billygoat's dinner, he's a-bed yond. Now this,' taking up another with six nicks ; ' is that divil Redhead's, and this,' seizing

a third with ten nicks, 'is Happy-Jack's. Well, thee
know'st he's got a bit o' beef; Redhead's nowt but taters,
he's a gradely brute is Redhead! and Billygoat's got a
pun or so o' bacon an' a cabbage. Now, thee sees, I've a
matter o' twenty dinners or so to bile every day, which
I biles in nets, an' if I dinna' fix 'em i' this rooad, I sud
ha' niver tell where to find 'em, and then there 'ud be sich
a row as niver yet was heer'd on.' Shortly afterwards,
Red Whipper came in, bringing with him a leveret. This
was a signal for Peg. His orders to her were, ' Get it
ready, and put it in along o' the rest; and look sharp,
or thee's head may be broken.' He then took off his
jacket and boots, and tumbled into a berth."

Such is a description of a shanty and of shanty life
fifty years ago. How does the system work now? Let
anybody go to an ordinary shanty on any line now in
progress, and judge for himself. The description of the
" shanty " just given answers very much to what is in
vogue at the present time. The sleeping accommodation
is somewhat, perhaps we may say decidedly, improved,
possibly the cooking, but I very much doubt whether
the moral aspect of affairs has. When talking with the
men on this question, a very frequent remark used to be,
" Well, to tell you the truth, sir, it's a regular hell on
earth when a lot o' chaps gits together on the drink, as
they does most evenings." I have had this positively
asserted to me that in a shanty where there was not
regular sleeping accommodation for more than eighty,
as many as one hundred and twenty have been known
to take refuge for the night. On inquiring how this
was managed, I was told this: " Why, just in this how,
the shanty-keeper rather than turn 'em out, not wishing
to lose his custom, gives 'em their choice, them as ain't
regular 'uns, whether they have bed, table, stool, or

floor; he charges 4d. a night for a bed, 1d. for a table or a form, and ½d. for the floor."

I have no doubt he might have added that a great number, having become so hopelessly drunk, take the floor of necessity. Should any of the readers of this chapter doubt the fact of the fearful licentiousness of the shanty system on the old principle, let him go into such a den on a wet day, when the men are unable to work, or, in fact, almost any evening on a week day, and any hour after 12 o'clock on Sunday, and he will no longer be inclined to doubt. Take an ordinary navvy settlement where there is no shanty of this description, and one where it is flourishing with all its evils, and you will soon see what the comparative state of the two settlements is. Ask any thoughtful observer of navvy life, and he will tell you that an ill-conducted shanty, as I fear the majority of shanties are, is a pestilential centre contaminating the whole colony. Whose fault is it? Indirectly it is the fault of those in authority, whose business it is to conduct the works. Yet they are not altogether to blame. Now, what happens? When any large works are about to commence, the wary shanty-keeper hears of it. He starts in good time to some out-of-the-way place perhaps, through which the line is to pass. His keen eye and shrewd sense of business soon observe where the men will congregate. He goes to the unwary local landlord (not to the contractor, often he is too sharp for that), and he rents a piece of land for a certain time. Just close to the huts, not on the company's land, he opens a " tommy shop." He next obtains from the unwary magistrates his license for the sale of intoxicating drinks, and hoodwinks the police. People begin after a year to grumble that such iniquities are practised near, and say, "We must put a stop to it." Nobody moves; things go on from bad to worse. Then everybody says, "Oh!

well, it's too late now, the works will be over soon." So
the matter goes on to the end. To say that this is the
history of every shanty and the mode of procedure with
every shanty-keeper would be unjust, but it, alas! is far
too common. Now, what should happen? Were I a contractor, the independent speculator should at all events
have to compete with me in making provision for the
accommodation of my workmen. Our leading contractors
are beginning to argue thus about the shanty system.
Men are drawn together from all parts of the country,
huts are provided, huts, too, which are often replete with
many comforts, but there stands the low shanty where
men like to herd together in numbers. Why should not
the contractor set up his rival? The others would then
soon cease to exist, and the result would be that steadier
workmen would be got together. Let there be in every
large settlement of navvies, as well as the contractor's
huts, the contractor's shanty. Let it be fitted up in such
a way as will give reasonable comfort to them, and, above
all, let it be conducted by good rules drawn up after careful thought, and be presided over by a man and woman
with assistants, who shall be responsible to the heads of
the firm, or their representatives, having no money
interest in the amount of *intoxicating* liquors they sell.
There are scores of men and women in the navvy huts
of England who could fill the post well, and make their
mates happy; and there are hundreds and thousands
of navvies, young and old, longing to lead a steady life,
who would thus gladly take refuge from the temptations
of the ordinary hut and shanty life. That shanties conducted on true principles would be a moral and even
financial success, I entertain no doubt. The men would
hail them gladly. At first, perhaps, they might be a
little shy, but the shyness would soon be overcome, and
the present gigantic evils in due course be overthrown.

Contractors, let me earnestly and very respectfully urge you to try it. It is not for me to dictate rules, but a code would soon be suggested by a committee of the workmen themselves, of whose experience and co-operation the authorities might easily avail themselves.

Already the movement has begun. The late Rev. L. M. Evans, whose labours amongst the navvies are so well known, thus describes in the "Quiver" a step in the right direction in Yorkshire:—

"There is one other building in our navvy village. It is one of the outliers, and is known by the name of the shanty. In other words, it is the public-house of the place, but it is under very strict rules. No spirits are sold here, only beer. It is open only at stated times, and for short periods. Sometimes it opens only to serve those who fetch the beer away, and in the evening it is open for an hour, and the men may go and sit there and drink their beer, but this is not allowed on Sundays."

Doubtless, there are many other places in which the evil is being remedied, and a better state of things consequently being brought about.

A well-conducted shanty is not all that is needed. In connection with it, or at any rate in the same settlement, there should be what is now popularly known as a "Navvy's Shelter." What such a shelter is, has recently been very graphically told by Mrs. E. Garnett, in an article entitled "Among Scotch Navvies," which appeared in "Good Words."

She says: "At Fairlie, in Ayrshire, the reader would find standing near the roadside, and close to the huts inhabited by three hundred men, employed in the construction of the new railway line which is being made there, two wooden rooms. And the object of this paper is to ask him to visit them with us. They have no pretensions to architectural beauty. They are just the buildings one commonly sees at navvy settlements, and what we should expect to find in the Far West or on the sheep-runs of Australia. They are built of planks, and the roofs and sides are covered with felting, which occasionally enjoys a bath of tar and sand. The two rooms are quite distinct, having different entrances and no communication between them, but for the sake of economy the middle wall acts as one side to both. They each have two ventilators, and are lighted by three side windows; and the far room has also a large window in one end. But our present object is to visit the room nearest to the high-road. We enter by a little porch, in which hang a jacktowel and a looking-glass, and where are arranged a tin washing-bowl, soap, and combs. We turn to the right, and enter the room itself—the first navvy shelter ever erected in Scotland. We find the windows are shaded by red moreen curtains, and the walls adorned with a clock, pictures, and two brackets, on which stand jugs of water and mugs.

"Exactly opposite to the door hang the rules of the shelter,—very simple and comprehensive ones,—framed and glazed, and above them a scroll with the motto of the place, in Gaelic and in English, 'Right ahead, lads!' The shelter is furnished with long tables, forms, a good stove, lamps, and a school-desk, wherein are kept 'useful sundries.' The end of the room is partitioned off, and makes a little home for a respectable man and his wife, she being the school-keeper. The room, therefore, though on the outside it measures about forty feet long, is shortened to twenty-four feet within; this seems to us a mistake, though we are told the arrangement was unavoidable. The object—as its name denotes—of this room is simply to provide a free place of shelter and comfort for the navvies; a place where they can sit, warm and comfortable, and smoke their pipes, read the

papers, of which there is a plentiful supply, and play
innocent games, as draughts, dominoes, &c.—a refuge,
in fact, from crowded huts other than the public-house."

We had a room attached to our Mission chapel at
Glaston very similar to this, and, as I have said elsewhere, a very useful adjunct we found it.

Connected with a navvy's shelter, there should be a
savings' bank, open on certain evenings, of which pay-day
should be one. Where such a large assemblage of men
is gathered, and so many hundreds of pounds paid in
wages, there would not be great difficulty in inducing the
post-office authorities to send over one of their representatives at least once a week.

A library, too, might be under the same roof. Properly
managed, these things would not entail much expense
beyond the fitting up of the room. An occasional
"gathering," or the proceeds of an entertainment now
and then, would keep the balance on the right side.
There is one other shelter—for, I suppose, the existence
of schools and little Mission churches—which is perhaps
more urgently needed than any. What we want in all
works is a separate building for an hospital. No one
knows, but they who have seen it, what the inconveniences of a crowded hut are for nursing purposes. A
manifestly serious accident is considered as a case for a
town hospital, and the patient, as a rule, is taken there at
once. But there are hundreds of cases of slight ailments,
apparently trifling wounds, which often develop into
long and serious illness, ending frequently in death. I
have dozens of instances in my mind. There is poor H.,
down at the turf huts; he was weak and sickly when
he came on the works. He catches cold in the pit,
inflammation of the lungs speedily sets in, it leaves him
a hopeless consumptive. For weeks he lies in that little,
low, damp room, in which there are four other beds, some

of which are occupied night and day. Some of his comrades come home the worse of drink. The noise of the
engine rushing close by and the excitement of the day
have kept the patient awake from morn till night. When
night falls, he vainly hopes to snatch a few hours'
refreshing slumber. Yes; his poor, weak, shattered nerves,
the close air, the brutish behaviour of his *drunken* com-
panions, all conspire to make night hideous. So the scene
is repeated day by day and night by night. It is true,
the landlady is like a mother to him, and " butty Jack "
as a brother, and the lodgers send in a savoury morsel for
" poor Harry." What he wants, poor lad, as well, is the
sweetness and light, the bright, cheerful quiet of a well-
ventilated room. God knows, " poor chap," his days have
been few, and perhaps very evil, but now he longs for the
peace, the quiet of the old village-home he left fifteen
summers ago. He is tired and weary of his hard, rough
life, and yearns with tears for " summat a bit more
homelike than this ere crowded hut. You know, sir,
landlady's very good, that she be ! and Dick and Jim an'
all on 'em—they does what they can for a mate, but it
ain't like as if they could do just as they would. It's
better nor I deserve, I know, but it ain't a place, be it,
sir ? for a chap as is soon got to die." So weeks and
months even go on. At length he dies, surrounded by
his mates doing all they can in their rough tenderness to
alleviate the agonies of his exit from this world to one
where, we hope, he is at rest.

I will not attempt to sketch the time from the death
to the burial, how the shrunken, emaciated form lies there,
still in the same room, under the white sheet. This is
enough. It will touch many hearts. It sickens me to
attempt a description of some of the last illnesses and
dying hours of men and women in some of the navvy
huts of this land. They are no places for sick and dying

folk, let them be never so lowly born, and never so sinful
in their lives. What we want to see is a hut hospital,
or better still, a cottage-home in some neighbouring
village presided over by a competent nurse. Houses are
generally very easily found in country districts for the
heads of the line, let me plead that the sick and the
suffering in the lower ranks, often crushed and bruised
at their work, should have a quiet shelter wherein to
recruit their exhausted strength and regain the use of
their limbs that are maimed. Such a home will soon
attract loving hearts and willing hands to forward the
good work and to cheer those who from time to time
would be brought under its roof. Where is there a navvy—
man, woman, or child—who would not gladly give his mite
to support such a home ? I know hundreds who would.
Let the experiment be tried, for it is worth a trial ; but
let it be tried fairly and generously.

Nine navvies out of ten, if asked to describe themselves, would do it in these terms : " We be fellows as
works hard, lives hard, drinks hard, lies hard, and dies
hard." Let us try and soften the asperities of their lives,
and alleviate the sufferings of their deaths in some such
ways as those I have indicated, and in doing it we shall
teach them much of what true Christian charity means.

There is in existence on the Dover and Deal Railway,
now in course of construction, a building which combines
a Mission room, a house for the missionary, a coffee-room,
and an hospital. T. A. Walker, Esq., the contractor, is
another of those who has the moral and spiritual welfare
of his men at heart, and who is always ready to minister
to their comfort. The building which he has erected is at
a settlement near the Dover end of the line. I am told
it comprises a Mission room, forty-two feet by twenty-
seven feet, a coffee-room of the same dimensions, both very
lofty ; between them is the Missionary's house, containing

sitting-room, kitchen, back kitchen, two bedrooms, and two other large rooms fitted up as the hospital. We need hardly say that a provision of this kind is much appreciated by the men and their families. All I have met speak of it in very glowing terms. May they soon be able to tell of such places on every important public work where men are thus gathered in crowds. It is a reform urgently needed, and one which, if carried out, would be most gratefully welcomed. The proof of this assertion may be found in the fact of the grateful and appreciative remarks of the men who have been fortunate to live on works where such agencies existed. The beer-selling portion of the community, of course, will, as a rule, oppose the new system at first, but they will see the advantage of it in time, and " come round."

CHAPTER VI.

SCRAPS AND CUTTINGS.

BEING much interested for a long time in the subject of navvy life, whenever I came across, in books or newspapers, any notice referring to the subject, I applied a pair of scissors to the paragraph and transferred it to my collection. I now give you a few such extracts and cuttings, which may prove interesting, and show some of the lights and shades of navvy life from other observers. The first is a love story, entitled—

" A ROMANCE IN HUMBLE LIFE.—The following slip from a newspaper has been sent us, but no mention is made whether it is Preston, Rutland, or Preston, Lancashire. A young woman in Preston whose physical deformity was compensated by remarkable industry and perseverance, won the heart of a good-looking navvy, who was engaged on the railway works now in progress there, and arrangements were made for the wedding; but a day or two before the day fixed for the wedding the prospective bride was taken ill, and died on the very day that the event was to have been celebrated. The navvy was inconsolable, and so scant were his means, that he could not afford to make himself presentable at the funeral, which he watched from the window of a public-house. The remainder of the story has a spice of romance in it. A short time before she was taken ill, a relative left her a sum of money, which to a person in her position would be regarded as quite a handsome fortune, but she did not acquaint her lover with this fact, probably intending it as an agreeable surprise after her wedding. But when her will was read, it was found that she had left nearly the whole of her money to her betrothed, who was at first unable to fully realise the change in his fortunes. He who a few hours ago was in poverty, and earning his livelihood at one of the most laborious occupations, may now be seen in the streets of Preston, dressed in the best, and evidently well to do in the world."

The next is anything but lovely! It shows what thousands and tens of thousands of navvies know too well, but they do not all profit by their knowledge, that drink is their especial curse. Possibly no mission work was being done among the unhappy men to whom this paragraph relates. It shows, too, the jealousy which often exists among the workmen of different nation-alities. These things are improving, but, alas! the amount of drunkenness and jealousy is appalling. Now, my friends among the navvies who read this, I hope you will say that this stigma of drink shall be wiped out as soon as possible. It looks very ugly, this title, doesn't it?—

"RIOTOUS NAVVIES.—On *Sunday* night a riot broke out amongst the navvies employed on the S—— and K—— Railway at R—— M——, near P——. It seems that the English and Irish residents in the huts, which are separated into 'nationalities,' fought, and each were in turn repulsed, wounded by the stones, &c., thrown. Superintendent W. and a body of West-Riding police from P—— were called to the scene. Several shots were fired in the affray; some twelve arrests were made. The navvies are said to have been *in liquor.* Several serious riots have before occurred at this cutting."

Now, this doesn't read at all well. Let us look through our collection and see if we can find something a little more attractive. Yes! here we are, just the very bit I wanted to find next. It is written by Mr. Smiles in his "Life of George Stephenson." By the by, you might save a few extra shillings which you spend on "beer" in the shanty, and buy the book itself: it would do you good; you would be better men for it. There are one or two others by the same author you would like; one is called "Self Help," another "Thrift;" then there's the

"Life of Telford." Buy these, and read them. Now for the story,—this time about English and French navvies, and, my boys, all to your credit!

In illustration of the working energy and powers of endurance of the English navvies, we may mention that when railway making extended to France, the English contractors for the works took with them gangs of English navvies, with the usual plant, which included wheelbarrows. These the English navvy was accustomed to run out rapidly and continuously, piled so high with "stuff" that he could barely see over the summit of his load the gang-board along which he wheeled his barrow. While he thus easily ran out some three or four cwt. at a time, the French navvy was contented with half the weight. Indeed, the French navvies on one occasion struck work because of the size of the English barrows, and there was an *émeute* on the Rouen Railway, which was only quelled by the aid of the military. The consequence was, that the big barrows were abandoned to the English workmen, who earned nearly double the wages of the Frenchmen. The manner in which they stood to their work was a matter of great surprise and wonderment to the French country-people, who came crowding round them in their blouses, and after gazing admiringly at their expert handling of the pick and mattock, and the immense loads of "dirt" which they wheeled out, would exclaim to each other, "Mon Dieu, voilà! voilà ces Anglais comme ils travaillent!"

There is no doubt about it, when a good honest English navvy sets to work, he *can* work; but many of them tell me they can work much better on oatmeal-water than beer. Oatmeal was extensively used on the Kettering and Manton line, and I never heard a man regret it yet.

I have a friend who is a doctor in the south of

England, and he writes to me, and tells me that twenty
years ago, the London and Brighton Company constructed
a new line to London, which passed through a district
where he was residing, and he received the appointment
of surgeon to the works. He gives some very interesting
reminiscences of navvy life, and he tells a striking story
about a navvy's rough sense of justice. I will give you
first an extract from his letter bearing on the subject of
"drink," and tell his story later on. He says, "The
navvy can absorb an enormous amount of beer. Some
cases of drink poisoning came before me, and when the
navvies elect alcoholic drink they soon succumb to its
effects, and 'delirium tremens' attacks them in the event of
any serious injury, and not unfrequently in very slight
wounds on the head. As a rule, they dislike the surgeon's
knife (who doesn't ?), and I invariably operated under
chloroform, the women of the huts being my assistants ;
and right well they behaved, displaying much courage
and aptitude where it was needed. I found many of the
men seriously inclined, but ever dreading the ridicule of
their associates, should they make an open avowal of
their better thoughts. These men cheerfully hailed the
efforts of our zealous pastor, and used their influence on
others in attending his special ministrations, but, alas ! a
rival—opening out in the shape of a beer shop immediately
opposite the hut in which they gathered on the Sunday
evenings—proved too strong an antagonist, and by degrees
all fell off ; and the few that otherwise would have held
on steadily could only be seen at the church occasionally."
Here, in these instances, you read of this curse of drink
leading to riot, to death temporal and spiritual.

I am afraid were all my notes and cuttings in this
chapter to be confined to the subject of drinking customs,
it would be a very long one, and were I to use all the
material at my command, I might fill a book with sad tales.

In old days, and not so very remote either, the drinking customs were abominable. Here is a horrible tale. A ganger, when the London and North-Western line was being made from London to Birmingham, actually proposed to raffle the dead body of a mate. Nearly 300 men joined the scheme at sixpence a-head, the raffle money to go towards a drinking bout. The narrator declares, " The raffle took place, so did the revel, but the funeral after a fortnight's delay was performed by the parish."

I thank God, from my very heart, those days are happily past. Still, even in connection with navvies' funerals, how often the amount of drink consumed is absolutely disgraceful ! I have known some few cases when the chief mourners have been nearly overcome with drink by the very grave side, and afterwards quite so. I have heard of many cases. But I bear my most grateful record that in this matter the men are improving. When it came to be our known wish, as it did after the first two or three funerals, that this custom should be broken, I must say that it was, as a rule, respected. Still, brother navvies, there is room for improvement. See your mates laid to their rest in such a state as you, if called at once to follow them, would not be afraid to go. This bad custom of drinking at funerals must be knocked on the head. It rests a good deal with the gangers. They generally collect subscriptions towards a funeral. Let them see that they are spent properly, and let no man give a penny without being satisfied that it *is* to go towards providing " a decent berryin," and not to an unseemly revel.

There are other drinking customs which must have a passing word. Alas ! again, their name is legion. I may pass by with a few words the foolish, and now happily-decreasing, custom of " colts " and " footings." These

taxes are often kept by the ganger, till there is a fair
sum together, and then there follows the usual scene at
the ganger's hut, generally on a Saturday night, or
Sunday morning.

An equally absurd and foolish custom is that known
amongst the "brickies" especially, as putting a man in
"the gauging-box." The alleged reason of the custom
is good enough, but the real end and object disgraceful,
because it only means an excuse for "a drink." If a
man breaks any of the traditional, or unwritten, code
of laws existing amongst his fellow-workmen, if he
breaks hut rules laid down by "the landlady," or com-
mits a breach of any of the laws of freemasonry, such as
it is amongst his class, a cry is raised, "Put him in the
gauging-box." A mock court is then constituted, a
judge appointed, and the offender is solemnly arraigned,
invariably found guilty, fined, often heavily, and his fine
either spent in a drink all round, or else put into an
accumulating fund till there is enough for a big drink on
a leisure half-day.

Now I ask you, men, and you who have more or less
the power in your hands, to put a stop to these excesses.
You gangers, time-keepers, foremen, and even you in
higher places, can anything be more prejudicial to the
successful, the skilled and efficient labour of the workmen, than these habitual and semi-authorised excesses?
These are public and well-known matters; but the secret
drinking is, if possible, still worse. There, I have delivered
myself strongly against these cursed customs inducing
men to their ruin; now I want to find something a little
more refreshing. I have repeated over and over again in
effect, that navvies are not a mass of immorality with no
redeeming points, for I believe that their nobler charac-
teristics outweigh the meaner. That there are men with
soft, loving, and sympathising hearts amongst them,

F

nobody who has had any experience amongst them can doubt. They are generous. A meal, "a night's lodge," a shilling or two, ay, even the contents of a "kit," are seldom refused to a mate, till he can find work to provide himself with the necessaries of existence. Many and many a pound goes, too, from the works, sent by some young navvy to his "old mother at home." They are capable too of right royal acts. Here is one. I will tell the royal story first, and then relate a noble act on the part of two navvies. Both stories are given in Smiles' "Self Help," in his chapter on "The True Gentleman." Quoting from Mr. Turnbull's excellent work on "Austria," he relates this anecdote of the late Emperor Francis :—

"At the time when the cholera was raging at Vienna, the *Emperor*, with an aide-de-camp, was strolling about in the streets of the city and suburbs, when a corpse was dragged past on a litter, unaccompanied by a single mourner. The unusual circumstance attracted his attention, and he learnt, on inquiry, that the deceased was a poor person who had died of cholera, and that the relatives had not ventured on what was then considered the very dangerous office of attending the body to the grave. 'Then,' said Francis, 'we will supply their place ; for none of my poor people should go to the grave without that last mark of respect !' And he followed the body to the distant place of interment, and, bareheaded, stood to see every rite and observance respectfully performed."

He continues in the following words :—

"Fine though this illustration may be of the qualities of the gentleman, we can match it by another equally good, of two English *navvies* in Paris, as related in a morning paper only a few months ago. One day a hearse was observed ascending the steep Rue de Clichy on its way to Montmartre, bearing a coffin of poplar-wood with its cold corpse. Not a soul followed, not even the living dog of the dead man, if he had one. The day was rainy and dismal ; passers-by lifted the hat, as is usual when a funeral passes, and that was all. At length it passed two English navvies, who found themselves in Paris on their way from Spain. A right feeling spoke from beneath their serge jackets. 'Poor wretch !'

said the one to the other, 'no one follows him; let us two follow! And the two took off their hats, and walked bareheaded after the corpse of a stranger to the cemetery of Montmartre."

These anecdotes are worth preserving, for they bring out most strikingly that in every grade of society you will find Nature's gentleman. This is my point. The navvy, in spite of his many failings and moral delin- quencies, will often be found to have the instincts of a true gentleman.

One day, while talking to one of our heroes on his mode of life, he began his story by telling me that he had led a regular romany (gipsy) life, but he "knowd how to behave his'sen when he got wi' a gentleman."

I pass on now to show that the navvy's life is of an exceedingly hazardous character, by reason of its expo- sure to danger. I do not know of a much *more* danger- ous life than that of a navvy. The paragraphs that follow well describe some of these dangers.

"'A sad accident happened last week on the A—— Railway. A gang of men were at work in a deep cutting, when the bank gave way, and several tons of earth fell on them. Almost all were more or less hurt, and some completely buried. Several bodies have been got out already, but it is feared there are more under the earth.' Who has not often read such news as this in the papers? A few years ago, when so many lines were being made, nothing was more common. Navvies! I don't suppose there is one of you who can- not call to mind some of his workmates who have been killed suddenly. 'Where's Jack So-and-so?' some one asks. 'Oh! he was killed when the bank fell in the W—— cutting,' is the answer. 'What's become of that Tom that used to be in your gang?' another inquires. 'Tom? Oh, poor chap, the engine ran over him and two more in the C—— tunnel. They hadn't time to say, "Lord, save us!" before they were cut in pieces.' My men! yours is dangerous work: there is but a step between you and death."

It would be very difficult to enumerate the varied causes of accident and death on a new line of railway.

Here is an account which in addition to its sad details
has "the spice of romance" about it.

"FATAL ACCIDENT ON THE RAILWAY.—On Saturday an inquest
was held at the Exeter Arms, W——, on the body of a navvy
named 'Jolly,' a single man, who was killed on the railway on
the previous day. C—— M——, railway labourer, deposed that
he was employed on the new railway works at Tilton-on-the-Hill.
'Jolly' worked in the same gang with him up to Thursday
week, when he (deceased) left the works. Had known him for
about four years, but never knew him by any other name than
that of 'Jolly.' Did not know where he came from. Had heard
him say he was fifty years of age. C—— B——, wife of a navvy,
said that deceased called at their hut a little after eight o'clock on
the previous Thursday, on his way to B——. He was sober.
G—— S——, an engine-driver in the employ of the contractor,
deposed that he left with his engine about twenty minutes to two
o'clock on Friday morning. It was then dark, and after running for
about five minutes towards F——, when they were in W—— cutting, he felt the engine lift as if it had run over something soft.
Witness then went back and found deceased, who was groaning.
He struck a light and found his leg was cut off and his bowels
protruding from the left side. He sent the fireman for assistance,
and ran himself to the huts, and when he got back, the man was
dead. The cutting at this point was very steep, and there was not
room for a man to stand between the face of it and the metals.
Witness was travelling five or six miles an hour. W—— B——,
fireman, gave corroborative evidence. G—— H——, a police-
constable, deposed to searching the body of the deceased. There
was nothing on him in the way of letters or marks on his clothes
to lead to his identification. Had heard that he came from B——,
near Devizes."

My next cutting is not particularly creditable, but it
is characteristic of the class. The doctor of whom I
spoke relates it in his reminiscences as an instance of a
rough sense of justice.

"There worked on this new line a man rejoicing in the name
of 'Cruiser,' of Herculean proportion, but withal a cur and a
bully, who most unmercifully beat another under his size. The
news reached an old friend of the sufferer, then working at Oxford,

on the Friday night. On the Saturday, after ' doing his bit,' he started from Oxford on foot, a distance roughly of sixty odd miles, and reached here on Sunday morning ; sought out ' Cruiser' and arranged a fight personally. He called in no seconds, the challenge coming in the shape of a straight blow after a few words of defiance before his mates. An adjournment was made to a neighbouring meadow, where Cruiser was soon convinced that a just cause in the hands of a less man and a true friend was not to be trifled with. Having revenged his 'chum's' wrongs, he washed his face, breakfasted off steak and fried onions, and coolly turned his steps towards Oxford, which he reached in time to appear at his post on Monday morning."

Pugilism is far less frequent than it was formerly. Sometimes now a disgraceful scene occurs, but I found no difficulty in putting a stop to a fight. Occasionally, a cur of a man of the bulldog type finds his way to a navvy settlement, and when this is the case, he is almost sure to foment what is usually known as a " row," inciting men to quarrel over the most trivial circumstances.

It is not often that navvies take to preaching, but here is a record of one who, to use the opening words of the paragraph, became

"THE HAPPY MISSIONARY.—The 'Register of Biography,' an offset of the ' Gentleman's Magazine' (vol. ii., 1869), gives, under the deaths of July 20th, the following obituary :—'At Chatham, suddenly, from heart disease, Peter Thompson, a street preacher, known by the *sobriquet* of "Happy Peter." The deceased, who was formerly a navvy, had latterly devoted himself to street preaching, in which it was stated he had been very successful, and had effected a great deal of good among many of the depraved classes in Chatham. On the evening of his death he was preaching to a large audience at the corner of one of the thoroughfares, the weather being intensely hot. He had just concluded his preaching with the word "Amen," when he was seen to stagger and fall, and on some persons going to him he was found to be dead.'"

Navvies are generally found very loyal subjects.

When the scare passed over the country about a possible war with Russia, and the Reserves were called out for drill, there was a large number working on various railways and other public works, and there was no hesitation about answering to the call. One day I was passing up " our line " and saw the ganger paying off some men. One fellow, as he left, shook hands with the man, saying, " Good-bye, Joe, I'll go and ' do my bit ' for my Queen and country, and then come back to ye agen." I do not judge from a single case like this, but, as a rule, it will be found that they are quite as well affected to the powers that be as other Englishmen.

PART III.

———◆———

CHAPTER I.

INTRODUCTORY.

A RECORD of the construction of the Kettering and Manton Railway, and of some of the phases of navvy life witnessed on it, would be very imperfect, if it omitted to give some account of the work of the Church amongst the railroad population there whilst the line was in progress. Many members of the congregations gathered together in the little Mission churches from Sunday to Sunday, and ofttimes in the week day too, would be sorely hurt and disappointed were no mention made of this Church Mission. It is against the dictates of modesty to say as much as might be said about the history of the Mission, since the writer of this sketch took a prominent share in carrying out the designs of those who planned the work, and his name would be constantly recurring. However, he cannot but record some of the leading features of the work, its lights and shadows, its joys and sorrows, and he must speak, too, of the more secular as well as the spiritual agencies employed to elevate, refine, and attract those with whom he had to deal. When the whole tale is told, it is only the history of a single attempt to begin a great work,

which we believe future years will see growing and
developing, and as it spreads, tending towards, and
finally accomplishing, the removal of the reproach which
seems to have settled on the navvy's head. Though
from the very nature of the exigencies of railway,
reservoir, dock and such like works, the shifting
character of the population, the brevity of its stay in
one place, the almost incessant shoals of workmen passing up and down, it would be hopeless to build up a
settled and permanent congregation; yet that infinite
good may be done by the efforts of the Church in the
midst of such a population cannot be doubted. For this
reason : wherever the Church goes with her message of
love and mercy, if that message is delivered with strong
faith and persistent zeal, men will be gathered in, and
souls won for the Master. It was in the strength of this
faith that our work was begun and carried out.

Anybody who had any concern for the soul of his
brother man, had he passed along the line in the early
part of the year 1876, must have acknowledged that
there was a pressing call for a separate and special
organisation to supply the spiritual needs of the larger
bodies of workmen who were beginning to congregate
here and there at intervals along its course. The various
clergy through whose parishes the line was about to pass
became anxious as to the effect these new visitors would
have upon their people, and still more anxious how to
supply the spiritual wants of which I have spoken.
Some doubted whether a special effort should be made,
independently of parochial organisation, but all at length
saw the necessity of "something being done." This
doubt and hesitation probably gave rise to the separate,
though harmonious agencies which were eventually
employed. Among the earliest efforts which were made,
were those at Gretton and Corby, in which parishes the

work first commenced. The Rev. A. White, Vicar of
Gretton, was enabled in the latter part of 1875 to
secure the services of an earnest-minded layman (Mr. W.
Chapman), who began at once to act as Lay-reader, con-
fining his ministrations to these parishes. Thus "The
Gretton and Corby Mission" had its beginning. Whilst
this effort was struggling into life, a similar movement
was going on in other districts, though little or nothing
was done to carry it into effect till the spring of 1876.
Between the autumn of 1875 and the summer of the
following year, mushroom villages had sprung up more or
less rapidly all along the route. Groups of huts, with
their picturesque surroundings, might be seen by this
later date at Wing, Glaston Fox Covert, Glaston Field,
Seaton, Gretton, Corby Wood, Oakley, and Rushton, but
of these, Corby was the only place where service was
regularly held till 1876. The men were first located
here in large numbers; here the first chapel was built;
and here, therefore, was the first call for work, and the
first response to it. All honour to those who undertook
the work, for which many who came within its influence
will be ever thankful! At Glaston, the then Rector
occasionally gave an evening service, but he met with
little encouragement, and he had not time to make much
headway before the want which was felt for a special
organisation was supplied. To this special movement
he gave his sanction and support in common with most
of the other clergy, acting as secretary till the time of
his death, an event which drew out much sympathy in
the neighbourhood and amongst the railway population.
It is of this effort, known especially as "The Bishop of
Peterborough's Railway Mission," that this account professes mainly to speak, for while the other Church
agencies had his countenance and support, it was the
district from Manton station to the borders of Gretton

parish where his original plan was carried out. Some account of its origin may be interesting to our readers.

Almost as soon as the new-comers began to appear in the county of Rutland, a conviction of the necessity of a special effort for their spiritual provision pressed itself on the minds of Churchmen who foresaw the extensive nature of the new undertaking. The first mention of the subject publicly (though the Bishop and the Chancellor had previously discussed it in private) was at a medical club meeting at the Uppingham Union House. At this meeting, the Chancellor and several of the local clergy and others were present. The bearings of the question were then talked over. After this, the matter seemed to languish, and there was a danger of a collapse; till the Bishop himself had occasion to visit the county on a Confirmation tour, and to pass through the midst of what was now becoming every day an increasingly busy scene of life. He made a point of visiting the works in company with the Chancellor and one or two others, and surveyed the field of action for himself; went back to Uppingham and discussed his plans, and threw himself heart and soul into the work of making the mission an accomplished fact. He at once caused a statement to be prepared, for which the contractors willingly furnished information, "for the purpose of showing the condition and number of men likely to be employed on the new line;" and this statement, together with a circular letter, was issued at once. We give the letter as it stands, showing, as it does, a true appreciation of the principle of the adaptability of our Church's system to the varying needs of various conditions of men. It is dated—

"PALACE, PETERBOROUGH,
June 7th, 1876.

"DEAR SIR,—May I entreat your earnest and favourable consideration of the accompanying appeal.

"The large and sudden influx of labourers employed upon the new lines of railway passing through many of our country parishes throws upon these, for some time to come, a burden for which their existing resources cannot be expected to provide.

" On the other hand, the presence of a labouring population of nearly four thousand souls in our midst calls for special effort on the part of the Church to provide them with the means of grace.

" It is unfortunately but too certain that they will not, of their own accord, resort to our parish churches in search of these, and that they need, therefore, some missionary agency which may bring the message of the Gospel to their homes.

" I am anxious, as suggested in the accompanying statement, which has been prepared at my request by a committee on the spot, to obtain for this purpose the services of at least two missionary clergymen and two lay readers, who should devote themselves to labouring amongst the 'navvies' and their families along the new line of railway from Rushton to Manton.

" I can only hope to obtain the necessary funds for this work by individual subscriptions, and I naturally make my first appeal to those who, either as owners of land along the line, or as share-holders in the railway, may feel that they have an interest in the spiritual welfare of the large multitude whom this enterprise is bringing amongst us.

" I venture, therefore, earnestly to entreat your assistance in the effort now being made on their behalf.—I am, faithfully yours,

"W. C. PETERBOROUGH."

Thus originated the Bishop's Mission, which has since caused him occasionally to be spoken of in some of the papers as " The Navvy Bishop," and by many of the men themselves as " *our* Bishop," a title which, probably, he will value even more than the former: as they thus declare that not only has their name attached itself to him, but better still, that he has attached himself and the Church of which he is an overseer to them. It must not be supposed that Bishop and clergy were the only people whose hearts were warm in the matter, though they naturally took the leading share in the work. The hearts of earnest-minded laymen were being moved, too, as they thought of those who were " as sheep having no shepherd."

Prominent amongst these laymen was one whose name in the earlier days of the works was a household word. The allusion is to one in authority on the works, but whose name, though suppressed, will be well known. Holding a position on the staff which gave him much authority, in every way possible he lent the weight of his influence and Christian character to the promotion of a scheme for which he had long prayed. When we lost him from the neighbourhood, we lost a firm supporter, and one who knew and felt the bad name which the lives of his men had when untamed by the humanising influences of the Gospel. Mainly through his instrumentality the matter was laid fairly before his chiefs, Messrs. Lucas and Aird, who had already given attention to the matter and were prepared to act. They did so with a readiness and generosity which calls for exceeding thankfulness ; of their share in the work it is impossible to speak with sufficient gratitude. They had brought something like 4000 souls into a comparatively limited area, and they nobly and without hesitation recognised their responsibility to respect their spiritual as well as their temporal claims and comforts. Besides subscribing a handsome annual sum of money to the Bishop's Mission Fund and the other organisations, they built Mission churches all along the line wherever they were needed, and instructed their agents to afford every practicable facility in carrying out the Bishop's plans. The instructions were most loyally attended to by the authorities at the central and outlying districts. A writer on Missions to Railway-men, in reference to the responsibilities of contractors in this matter, makes use of the following words. "'But surely,' our readers will say, 'the employers will see to this.'

" Yes, so they should, but as a rule, to which there are noble exceptions, as Messrs. Lucas and Aird, they do not.

Bare toleration is all that is scarcely conceded on some works."

It was, therefore, a matter of heartfelt gratitude to those concerned, that the contractors did not give a merely cold and an indifferent sanction, but a thorough and earnest co-operation, and, what was more, evinced an increasing interest. Happily, to these names, there may now be added several others in connection with other railway missions. With such favourable conditions, the Bishop's plan assumed definite shape; his appeal resulted in drawing out many liberal promises of help; and he was enabled in July to appoint a clergyman to the work. The Bishop's intention, as will be seen by a reference to the letter of appeal, was to have made the whole course of the line, with the sanction of the various incumbents, a temporary extra parochial mission district, with a staff of clergy and lay readers employed under the same organisation. With a view to carrying out this scheme, my residence was fixed .at Gretton as a central spot. However, the plan in its entirety was not adhered to, as far as the Kettering end was concerned, as those who employed the layman, already at work, decided that his work should be carried on under their immediate supervision; and the smaller population in the few huts beyond the Corby district were ministered to by another layman, generously supported by one of the landowners in that neighbourhood, to whom he held himself responsible. These arrangements brought about three separate missionary agencies, occupying three distinct sections of the line, viz., "The Bishop's Mission," "The Corby and Gretton Mission," and "Sir W. de Capell Brooke's Mission." Besides these, it should be mentioned that the Midland Company sent a Scripture reader, who held a roving commission all along the line, and did much good amongst those who, perhaps, were not otherwise reached. It is to be regretted that these various agencies were not merged, though, happily, all worked harmoniously. The great needs which were pressing heavily at all centres allowed no time to be lost in the discussion of the division of territory, or trifling questions of jurisdiction. The workmen and their families had arrived; they were crying out for help; the only thing to be done was to set to work at once to supply it; for it was clear to us all that they were only like birds of passage; and it was manifest to those who had the work at heart that no time was to be lost over mere formalities; so we said in effect, "Let us join hands together and work to bring these wandering souls to Jesus." No sooner were the areas of operations defined than the missions began to make themselves felt all along the line.

It is "The Bishop's Mission" at Glaston, Seaton, and Wing to which this account will be mainly confined, as the writer has not space to enter fully into the whole history and working of the others, though he is permitted to record their successful issue, and to look back to many scenes of encouragement and happiness in connection with them.

Now for a few words of necessary autobiography. When it was clearly arranged that the large railway populations at the three places already named should be the objects of my care, I removed my quarters to Glaston, the centre of the now more contracted field of labour. Here I was enabled to pitch my tent on a hillside close to the railway huts, and in the very centre of the three little "wooden towns" so rapidly increasing in inhabitants. A more convenient spot could not easily have been selected, or more generously offered, than the welcome shelter of the vacant farmhouse, which you must be good enough to substitute for tent. In this house, "The Lodge," as it was called, one of the happiest periods in my life was spent. Doubtless, many of the workmen will remember where it stood, and sometimes think of the many conversations some of us held together in it. Here it was that I brought my bride in the summer of 1877, where we found a true "navvy's welcome" awaiting us, which will always be remembered as we look at a handsome clock which graces the chief chimney-piece of our home. This is an almost necessary digression; we must now go back to the commencement of the Mission.

For the first six months the work was carried on single-handed, and it was found very difficult, indeed well-nigh overwhelming, for one man to attempt to cope with the multiplication of duties which lay before him. Consequently it was a matter of great rejoicing when a true fellow-helper was found in Mr. John Bruster, a zealous layman, who had been recommended as having already done good service for the Church. His work was destined to lie principally at Seaton, and in January 1877 he commenced his labours in that district. His name will be long and affectionately remembered by many old friends far away. A more loyal fellow-yokeman could not well have been found. To him and those gathered round him most of the good work done in that place is mainly due, though we at Glaston took our share and interest in its progress. Whatever has been done for good, to God be all the praise! Our object has been to sow the good seed of the Word of God, in humble reliance on Him, never feeling so much as now the truth of the Apostle's dictum, that a Paul might plant, an Apollos water, but that God alone could give the increase. The work has indeed been mainly a sowing of seed. The "bread was cast on the waters," and we hope, were it after "many days, to find it."

It is not intended here to make any analysis of spiritual results, even though such should be possible, in the records of a number of individuals, who by the agency of the Mission have openly "professed the faith." Thank God, we could give a list of many names of young and old alike who have become through it true disciples of the Lord Jesus. Many a time since have our hearts been encouraged by letters we have received from those who have left the works, writing from various parts of the United Kingdom, and in two or three cases even from foreign lands, whither they have now wandered. These letters, very many of them at any rate, breathe a spirit of thankfulness that the writers of them came under the influence of the Mission, and express a determination to try and keep "steadfast in the faith." Some of them tell of difficulties and doubts, some speak of failure, some ask for guidance. That many, one scarcely dare think how many, have come and gone with their hearts apparently unmoved, is, alas, too true a fact. There may still have been a silent influence at work which will one day effect a mighty change in their condition. That God alone knows: to Him we confide them. His "Word is like a hammer." Wielded by some other missioner on some other and future mission field, a blow from it may strike again, and break the heart already bruised and shaken. The seed sown has sprung up so unexpectedly in some cases, falling, though we feared it did, on some hard and stony heart. We might, if need be, refer to the offertory test. The men gave most liberally to the support of various Mission agencies.

One Christmas morning, a few workmen and their wives and little ones gathered together in one of the Mission chapels to keep their Saviour's birthday. They were only a few that happy morning, so few that one's heart sank to think there should be so many living near, and *only* these who cared to come. How many of those few were touched, cannot be known: there was one at least. Passing by, and hearing the sound of praise, the man of whom we speak was attracted. He drew near and entered as we were singing " While shepherds watched their flocks." This was the first time, so far as we know, that he came. Afterwards, at irregular intervals, he joined the congregation worshipping there, very often not coming for a month or two together. One almost began to despair of him, as of many others: so strikingly attentive was he when there, and yet so strangely irregular. At last the test came. Sickness laid him low. We knelt in a rude hut by his dying bedside, and I shall never forget him, as, with tears streaming down his cheeks, he said in broken utterance, " Ah, sir, that was a blessed Christmas morning for me when I came to your chapel; I have thought of that hymn you were singing many and many a time since then." The strong frame of that man wasted day by day; but as his body grew weaker, his faith seemed to gain daily increasing strength. At length, borne down with agonising pain, he passed away to his rest. It was instances like this, and not a few either, that helped to keep up one's courage and to strengthen hope. Letters, too, as I have said, from one or another who had long since left the " works," brought words which gave comfort. One who had been very regular at our services wrote to me from a foreign land, and said : " I was glad to hear of the service in the tunnel, and to hear about the hymns which were sung ; me and —— very often enjoy ourselves by singing the same and others which we used to sing at G——, and we get plenty of coloured company (meaning natives) while we sing." So those men who came under the influence of the Gospel and learnt its power, became, in a sense, missionaries themselves. Were it desirable, I could give extracts from many letters which show that the new and better life of the Christian was beginning to make itself felt in the heart of even the much despised and uncivilised "navvy;" but I have no right, without permission, to make public what were intended to be letters from a friend to friend.   We must now proceed to tell how we made progress, and to record other reasons for encouragement.

CHAPTER II.

NOTES OF PROGRESS.

I MUST confess I was somewhat puzzled when the time came for me to make an actual acquaintance with my new flock. I did not consider they were merely so many " strong beasts, with a big swallow for beer," but that they were my brothers. So I thought the best thing to do was to show them what my thoughts really were; and when we came to talk to one another, we found that we had very much in common. A friendly shake of the hand with one, a chat with another, a little while in this hut and a little while in that, soon brought us together. Now and then a visit to the cutting, a climb up the bank, and an occasional trip into the tunnels taught me much about " Navvy Life " in a few weeks. As a rule a working man gets on best with somebody who takes some interest in his actual work, and my new friends and I often held parley about their different occupations, and had many a long discussion about this job and that. They used to teach me a very great deal, and this they knew, and in consequence they were quite as ready to learn on their part. I can't quite tell you how it was, but we seemed to get friendly from the very first, although we didn't say very much about religion at all, to begin with. They were not long, however, before they knew perfectly well what I had come for, and I cannot say that they received me with any the less personal kindness on that account, for though our navvy friends as a rule are supposed to have no special concern for religion, or to be righteous overmuch, they are always very respectful, and frequently very attentive, to a clergyman. I never yet was insulted by a navvy, and the only man we ever had forcibly to eject from any of our Mission or reading rooms, was a reprobate huckster from a neighbouring village, who, I suppose, would, in his more sober moments, have affected to look down on the navvies.

But the questions we have before us just now are, How our Mission work progressed ? and, How we set about it ? I have attempted in previous pages to give some idea of the great engineering undertaking in the construction of the line. It is more difficult to survey and report on our Church work. A few thrusts from a navvy's spade will soon make a very visible effect on unbroken ground, but a great many cuts from the Gospel sword do not always produce such an immediate and *visible* result ; so I find it hard to chronicle results and to tabulate spiritual victories as one would compute the accomplishment of manual labour. I caution my reader once more not to expect an analysis of spiritual results, but rather the means and modes by which these desired results were most likely to be produced. When I arrived at Glaston, I found that a large number of people had already clustered thickly from Manton station all along my new district. The contractors had already built chapels at two of the more thickly populated places, but as yet no effort had been made at Seaton, and at Glaston scarcely any of the railway people came to a service which had been held three or four times for their benefit. So a new start had to be made. I conducted my first service on Sunday afternoon, August 20th, at Seaton. Several of the engineers and foremen were present, including Mr. Priestley, who read the appointed lesson. There were also a good many children. Altogether, including men, women, and children, I find by a reference to my diary we numbered forty-two. Among these were only two *bonâ fide* navvies, one of whom I regret to say had imbibed so freely previously, that he accompanied the service with a series of running comments which were not the most appropriate, nor yet particularly edifying. However, I must give him the credit of candour, for, referring to a remark I had just been making, he exclaimed in the midst of my address, "that he had heard that in prison afore now." The result of our friend's determination to reflect aloud, was, that we had to take him quietly by the hand and lead him to the door, a process which he did not at all resent, though, of course, he continued his incoherent comments as he proceeded on his way. To tell you the truth, I thought this incident a strange beginning, and I rather wondered how often the process was likely to be repeated. Serious thoughts at once crossed my mind of instituting a new order of church officers, whose special duty it should be to prohibit the entrance of men in a similarly unsatisfactory state of equilibrium. The need never arose, as this was almost the only occasion we suffered any annoyance of the kind, for, happily, I found it to be one of the most stringent moral codes of the men not to allow their mates to go to a place of worship whilst under the influence of drink, and very seldom was this rule violated. Another digression this. Now to return. This service was on the whole encouraging. Though it attracted but few comparatively of the men it was intended to attract, yet it drew out the help and sympathy of the officials of the line, which was a great point gained, as these, in due course, brought in many of the "right sort," and contributed very decidedly to the success of the undertaking. The hymns we sung that first Sunday afternoon were "All people," "Rock of Ages," and "Sun of my Soul," to which I played the air on a small harmonium I had brought with me on the previous Saturday.

When our introductory service at Seaton was concluded, we extended our missionary journey two miles farther north-west, and halted at the settlement at Glaston. Here we went round to beat up a few recruits, but with little success. We only mustered seven, children and all told, including the storekeeper and his wife (Mr. and Mrs. Hilling), whose names will always be intimately associated with the history of the Mission, and who never missed a single service, week-day or Sunday, from that day to the closing service in that district. Always ready, always willing, ever obliging, the self-sacrifice of this estimable couple will not easily be effaced from the memories of those whose happy lot it was to share the many devotional exercises, in what will be remembered by us as "the Mission Cathedral." These two were of the very few who completed three years' residence in the district. The service at Seaton in the afternoon was enthusiastic compared to this. Seven people on two short benches in a corner of a building calculated to hold two hundred was not a particularly cheering sight. But the number was *seven*, and it brought with it its encouraging lessons, and its sacred symbolism was not forgotten. After the services at each place we tried to persuade those who were present to bring others the next Sunday, and this persuasion had some effect. How strange the contrast to the services in which it had been my privilege to take a share for some three years previous to my appointment to the charge of this Mission, in a grand old church, with all its fittings good and beautiful, with its large congregations and reverent ritual. The surroundings and experience of this Sunday's service were so strangely unnatural, that there was quite a struggle in my heart between courage and despair; but courage strove and won the day. The surroundings might have appeared more natural had the scene been laid in the backwoods of Canada, or on the hillside of a lately-acquired colony only just peopled with English residents. In a home county of England it seemed hardly possible. Four bare, *very* bare walls, and a few benches of the plainest of deal rendered the interior of the chapels uninviting. The hut in which the settlers lived, with its bright trappings and homely look, was much more inviting than the chapel in which they were to worship. However, it was one of our earliest efforts to make the chapels more fitting for the object for which they were erected. The bare fact of their existence at all was a matter for exceeding thankfulness, and they soon became the central buildings of the hut groups in more senses than one.

This Sunday saw the opening of the campaign at " our end," and an active spiritual force was now at work all along. Having made a beginning, much anxious thought was bestowed on future modes of action. One thing clearly must be done : there must be stated times of service. Nothing is so fatal as irregularity in the hours of service, and yet nothing so likely to prove attractive as *additional* and irregular services. So, though the hours were fixed, when it was known for an absolute certainty, as far as in this life there could be such, that we should be at our post, yet a surprise service was often organised in various places about the works. It was arranged that regular services should be given, and these services were notified in a way which could not be mistaken.

The exteriors of the chapels were soon to be distinguished from the huts which surrounded them by their little wooden steeples or turrets, and regularly every settler heard, or might have heard, the single bell chiming out its summons to prayer and praise. This was a simple thing, but it told on the people. The steeple made the building look a little different from its neighbours, and the bell it carried spoke with a voice every Sunday which all were obliged to hear, whether they heeded or not. To the careless, distance may lend a dreamy enchantment to the sound; but when the voice comes nearer, it speaks with a plainer message. The distant sound of the village bells could be heard over hill and dale at most of the huts, but they did not speak with the same distinct tones which the little chapel bell did, right in the midst of the dwellings of our navvy friends. I am a great believer in the power of a bell, and certainly many were attracted by the sound of those we set up.

Do not be alarmed if I add banners to bells, for we must first attract and then teach. Not satisfied with the power of the bell in all cases, we had resort to the banner. This is how it came about. One Sunday, and a very hot day it was, we were travelling across country to one of the distant Mission stations, when as we neared it we came across a group of stalwart fellows lying lazily outstretched, half in sun and half in shade, under one of the hedgerows in a country lane where four cross roads met. And as the chapel bell was then going, we gave our usual invitation to them to accompany us to the service, reminding them at the same time that it was Sunday. One of the group, who took upon himself the office of spokesman, in reply, said to us, " Ah! us chaps doesn't know Sunday from workaday, only us thinks on it sometimes when that there bell goes." Of course, that was only an excuse. So I said to him, " You shall know another Sunday in good time what day it is, if you will look out at the hut door towards the chapel, for I will have a flag put up." This incident reminds me of a story Robert Stephenson used to tell of the clergyman of a parish near Rugby, when the navvies

were making the Kilsby tunnel. He went one day to
the foreman of one of the gangs, and spoke of the fact
that he allowed his men to work on Sundays. But
one of the gangers, who was no better than the men
themselves, gave him a very characteristic answer, " Why,
Soondays hain't cropt out here yet ! " So *our* friend
seemed to think. True to our word, in a short time
three large flags could be seen floating in the breeze
every Sunday, from early morning till the shades of night
fell. We secured the longest scaffold poles we could
find on the works, and soon our most stalwart and
staunchest friends planted one securely in the ground
close by the porch of each of the chapels. The design
of the flag was a large red cross on a white ground.
These flags were exceedingly useful in attracting the
attention of new-comers to the existence of the chapels.
" What's the meaning of yon flag, Bill, or Jack ? " was
a query often put, as the new lodgers looked out on a
Sunday morning. " Oh, our parson puts it up to remind
us it's Sunday, and churching goes on up there once or
twice a day. I reckons it's a very good thing to let us
know like, and it's drawed a good many blokes in ; so
they tells, and I thinks some day as I shall go too, for
they tells me there's often a sight o' folk, and I can often
hear 'em a-singing as I stand here. My missus and two
or three of our lodgers are regular took up wi' it. What
do you say, mate, to goin' next Sunday ? "

The sight of the flags with the sign they bore often
encouraged us too. Travelling along the whole Mission
district of seven miles, there was no point at which you
could not see the sign floating above one or other of the
Mission stations, clearly reminding us of the work to be
done for the Master there. Whilst writing on this
subject of exterior and minor attractions, I ought to
mention that our chapel at one of the centres was care-

fully and doubly whitewashed, to mark it out from the rest of the huts which were coated with gas tar.

The interior, too, had to be made a little more inviting. The little chapels were soon, by the kindness of friends and by aid from our Mission fund and offertory, fitted up in a homely but churchlike style. At one end the Altar was raised on a little platform, and the hangings on the wall behind served to bring it into due prominence. The walls and cross-beams were brightened with appropriate texts in white letters on scarlet ground, which had a bright and cheery look. At one chapel, notably, the windows were soon filled with bright flowers, which helped us greatly, for the navvy is a child of nature, roving and free, and loves a " pretty posy." On the great festivals, too, we made as liberal a use of flowers as our supply would allow. In these simple but telling ways we gained a great point; the wooden hut looked more like what it was intended to be, the chief hut in the settlement; a tabernacle for the wandering tribe, " The Navvy's House of Prayer."

As the autumn sun began to decline earlier and the shades of night drew in more rapidly, we found it was necessary to add to our fittings means for lighting. Accordingly numbers of lamps were purchased, sufficient to throw a flood of cheerfulness over the room. I am a believer in the power of light. Every place of worship ought to be brightly lighted. To come from a cheerful and well-lighted house to a gloomy church at once depresses the spirits. I shall not easily forget the bright line of the chapel windows throwing out their cheery rays across the fields in which the huts stood. " Sweetness and light " are often spoken of together, and the proverb that " Cleanliness is next to godliness," is well known. One of the most marked features of the chapels was their cleanliness. Though they were frequently crowded at night, yet those whose duty and pleasure it was to keep them clean, always took a pride in doing so. Anybody who went into Glaston chapel at eight o'clock on Sunday morning must have been struck by its singularly neat and tidy appearance. Had you gone into the chapel on the previous Saturday you would have learnt the secret, for you would have seen one or more of the dwellers in the huts working like Trojans "to clean up things a bit for Sunday." The manner in which these facts were appreciated by the congregation will be better understood, as, from a local paper, you read how—

"A very interesting event took place in the reading-room in connection with Glaston Mission Chapel on the 27th of September. A number of the members of the congregation met together to make a presentation to Mr. and Mrs. S. Hilling, in recognition of their unceasing attention to the wants of those who meet together to worship in the chapel. Mr. Hilling has acted as one of the chapel wardens, librarian, Sunday-school teacher, and in various other ways been a true friend to the church. To his wife, the neat and cleanly appearance of the chapel and its fittings is mainly due. The proposal to present them with a Family Bible and an electro-plated teapot was very warmly taken up, and subscriptions flowed in at once from many railway people and others to provide for the cost of the articles, which were both very elegant. The presents were acknowledged with much emotion, and Mr. Hilling returned heartfelt thanks for himself and his wife for the kindness which had been shown them, and said that what little they had done was from a sense of duty. We hope they will both live long, and be as useful as they have been at Glaston."

Having described a few of the more noticeable features in connection with the general appearance of the chapels, I must proceed now to speak of the services. For the first few Sundays our service consisted of a few selected prayers from the "Book of Common Prayer," two or three hymns, a short passage from Holy Scripture, and an extempore address. After two or three Sundays we found that a regular form of simple prayers was desirable, and began accordingly to use a " Short form of Mission Service," specially sanctioned by the Bishop. This was compiled from the Book of Common Prayer, with special psalms which were used every Sunday. The lesson was selected at the discretion of the clergyman conducting the service, and his address was usually founded on some portion of it. For some time we used four hymns printed on a slip of paper, till we got the halfpenny edition of the S. P. C. K. Hymn-book, which served our modest requirements for some few months more. However, in the matter of hymns we were not easily satisfied, as we rather prided ourselves in the few we did sing, that we sang them heartily, and we were very desirous to learn more. Soon the kindness of the late Sir H. W. Baker enabled us to satisfy our wants, and in all our chapels we " adopted " to use the correct phrase, " Hymns, Ancient and Modern," and we found a practically inexhaustible fund of popular hymns and tunes. Perhaps somebody will inquire how with a shifting congregation we secured congregational singing. Our secret lay in this—we made the congregation the choir. First of all, a number of young men and lads were collected, and for a time we managed to keep them together; but in the course of a few months almost all of them left the works, either for other sections of the line, or more generally for distant parts of the country. As we watched the numbers getting thinner at the choir practices, our mistake dawned on us, and we determined to give up a regularly constituted choir, and to ask those of the congregation who cared to stay after the service to do so, and to practise a few hymns for the next service. A large number, especially in the winter months, accepted the invitation, and very happy were the hours which were thus spent. Sometimes before singing I would speak to them, when I could, of something interesting about the hymn, occasionally explaining it; sometimes I would tell

them who the composer of the hymn or tune was, with
any interesting episode in his life. When we set to
work to learn a new tune, we seldom failed to master it
in a rough way, though we had to go over the ground
a good many times. There was almost sure to be some
one present who knew something about music, and had a
correct ear and good voice, and so we got on. Many old
members of church choirs, with the memory of their
former happy days still haunting them, used to find their
way into the chapels, and frequently respond to the invitation to stay. I have met on the works with old chori-
sters, for instance, from York-Minster, Malmesbury, the
Leeds parish church, and a few other noted churches,
besides some of less renown. Often when I drew
out the history of a man as I chatted with him on the
road at night, or when sitting down alone beside the line
at his mid-day meal, I found that he had been a regular
church-goer in his earlier days; and not unfrequently I
heard such a tale as this, "Why, bless you, sir, if you'll believe me, I know I doesn't look much like it now, but when
I were a boy, me and Jack J——, him as works over on
Moss's job yonder, us used to go regular up in the singing gallery and sing wi' 'em. I've forgotten most on it
now, but sometimes one of our old tunes comes across me
and it sets me a thinking. Then there were two of my
sisters and one of his'n as used to join; they's married
now and settled down, but them *was* happy days, and I
often thinks I should like 'em o'er agen."

We seldom had less than four hymns at a service, and
we always began with one. It always seemed to bring the
people in good time, as they never liked to miss a "bit of
singing." By and by we learnt a few simple chants, but
though our rendering of the appointed canticles was hearty,
we found more difficulty in making them so thoroughly
congregational, owing to the "pointing," which must

always be more or less a stumbling-block to a constantly changing body of worshippers.   Some of the most popular hymns were "I was a wandering sheep," "A few more years," "Art thou weary?" "How sweet the Name," "We love the place."

As we made progress in the service of praise, so, too, we advanced in the service of prayer.   The short Mission form was in time alternated with the Litany, and, when after about twelve months the congregations had become as much settled as we could hope.them to be, we used occasionally the ordinary morning, and regularly the evening prayers, which soon became much appreciated and were entered into with as great a degree of heartiness as the shortened form.   As time progressed, we were enabled to announce celebrations of the Holy Communion, and though the attendance was but small, yet there were always a few.   Our special sphere of Mission work in the short space of time during which we could, in most cases, exercise an influence, was more especially that of reclamation and conversion than that of edification, for generally no sooner had we got to know something of a man's life and state, than we found he either had left, or was about to leave, the works.   At least this was so in seven cases out of ten, I should say.   A large number of children were brought for Holy Baptism from time to time.   By degrees we discovered many unconfirmed, and we prepared and presented them.   In short, so far as the circumstances of our rambling flock permitted, we endeavoured to adapt the Church's system to the wants of the Church's wandering, but not unfriendly children.

CHAPTER III.

RED LETTER DAYS.

THESE, it is hardly worth while to mention, were not sufficiently numerous to make a very long chapter. A child of scarcely three years is not likely to have experienced many marked days, still it has a few. Every nation has its festivals, every country its seasons of special mark, so every town and village. Every individual, too, for the matter of that. The Bishop's Mission had some such seasons which call for special record. I suppose I must reckon the day, to which I have referred in a former chapter, on which we held our first service as a sort of birthday festival, which was kept with becoming acts of remembrance when the second year came round. By the time of the third anniversary we had nearly all packed up our bag and baggage and left, and the chapels been submitted to the auctioneer's hammer, or taken to other works. The opening of the chapel at Wing demands a few passing words. Although the Mission commenced in 1876, we had only two chapels, one at Glaston, and the other at Seaton, till the following year. For some months the colony at Wing was not considered of sufficient importance to require its own chapel. Before the end of the first year the population increased considerably, and for some months we held service where we could—now in the common living room of one of the huts sometimes in the pay office, often on the slopes of the railway bank, and for several Sundays in the summer we pitched a tent, kindly supplied by the contractors, and held service in that. At first we had no seats, so the congregation used to sit or kneel on the grass. Very often several men would come and lie at full length in one corner of the tent and listen ; sometimes they would gather shyly round the outside where they could hear. We found singing and speaking under canvas rather difficult, but we were glad of the shelter, as we were then sure of a congregation in all weathers. However, this state of things did not last long, for in the autumn of 1877 we had the satisfaction of seeing an old hut from Corby Wood being drawn up the hill towards Wing to be erected as a temporary church. Before the hill top was reached, the waggon which bore the load broke down, and it seemed as if we were to be doomed to disappointment, and to observe our feast of taber- nacles a little longer. But orders had been given at head-quarters that a chapel was to be erected, and soon it was standing with its little turret and open porch under shelter of the hill at Wing cross-roads. A disused hut, as you may readily imagine, wanted a con- siderable amount of renovation before it became fit for a house of prayer. This was soon done ; and though much less churchy in its interior appearance than the others, still with a few pictures, texts, and hangings at the " east end," which, by the way, happened to be south-west, it looked very neat and fitting for the use to which it was now appropriated. We held our first service there the last Sunday in September, making it a kind of Harvest Festival, and from that day till the end of 1878 regular services were held there. The occasion of the opening of this chapel was certainly a red letter day to us, who scarcely knew from Sunday to Sunday, till we got our tent, where the service should be held. To enumerate all the minor days of importance to the Mission, would be only to weary our readers, and to make a formal list of preachers' names and the dates of their coming amongst us. Every Lent, as it came round, though it may seem strange to say so, was the scene of a series of red letter days to the men and their families, for we had arranged for special Mission services once a week, securing for this purpose some able preacher, generally from a distance. Taking all these special occasions into account, we had no less than twenty-five different clergy, either Bishops, Priests, or Deacons, to address the congregations during the progress of the Mission. Many a stirring and earnest word was heard from each and all of these, not yet forgotten, let us hope, in many cases.

We now proceed to give an account of the more important of these occasions. Episcopal help was most willingly afforded us. As I have already recorded in a former chapter, our own Bishop was early on the spot reconnoitring the ground and drawing up a plan of action; but circumstances prevented his visiting the line again till some months had elapsed after the actual opening of the campaign. Meantime a happy event occurred, and Sunday, 12th September 1877, is a day long to be remembered. The Bishop of Lincoln, who was staying in the neighbourhood, kindly consented to give an address at the Glaston Mission Chapel. The service, which was held in the evening, was very bright and hearty, and there was a large congregation of the work-people and their families, besides some few from the neighbouring village. The Bishop adapted himself to his audience in a wonderful manner, and gave a very touching and eloquent address from Isaiah xl. 1–8, laying special stress on the words, "The voice of him that crieth in the wilderness, Prepare ye the way of the Lord, make straight in the desert a highway for our God. Every valley shall be exalted,

H

and every mountain and hill shall be made low, and the crooked shall be made straight, and the rough places plain; and the glory of the Lord shall be revealed, and all flesh shall see it together." He spoke to the men in stirring language, using abundant and graphic illustrations from the varied character of the works, telling them plainly but lovingly of some of their "rough places" and "crooked ways." Once he spoke in most touching simplicity for some few minutes to the young. Indeed his words seemed to come home with vivid force to old and young alike, as he in turn addressed the various classes who were ranged before him. The earnest tones and venerable form of the Bishop, as he stood habited in a large old-fashioned surplice formerly belonging to Dr. Cookson, with huge sleeves and collar, without hood or stole, seemed somehow to carry one back in thought to the early days of the Christian Church. On the following day he expressed a wish to see something of the works, and made an excursion along the temporary line in an open truck drawn by an engine. He was attended by his son, to whom the Mission is in so many ways indebted, the Rev. Chr. Wordsworth, Rector of Glaston. The Mission staff and several of the engineers and others also went with him. The Bishop spoke to many of the men individually, and took a great interest in all that was going on. The visit of the great Bishop was a happy accident, but one which we record with deep thankfulness, as many we believe were seriously impressed by it.

Not many weeks had passed by before the promised and anxiously-expected visit from the Bishop of Peterborough became an accomplished fact. He himself, as he told us, had been looking forward to it for a long time; and when he came he showed that he meant work, and he mapped out a very full day. Having already had the privilege of the presence and encouragement of one

Bishop, we were very anxious that our men should have an opportunity of hearing and seeing him whose name is a household word in England. Our privilege this time was not for a brief hour, but for a whole day. The Bishop arrived at Bisbrook Hall on Saturday evening, 20th October, where he was the guest of those untiring friends of the Mission, to whom we shall ever be grateful—the Hon. W. C. Evans-Freke and Lady Victoria Freke, who spared neither time nor money to help on the cause, and whose generous hospitality often cheered us after a weary day's labour. On the morrow, Sunday, October 21st, the Bishop had arranged that Mission services should be conducted at each of the chapels, and due notice was given to the workmen. I remember being much amused, and puzzled too, when, as on the previous Friday, I went down to one of the cuttings where thirty or forty men were at work, and invited them to come to the service, one fellow said to me as I was crossing some scaffolding with a view to return up the bank, "I shall come, master, for I've had a goodish bit to do with Bishops in my time. I had a Bishop for my godfather, and what's more, I've rode in a carriage with an Archbishop." He wouldn't give me the key to the puzzle that day, but I discovered subsequently that his father had been in some service connected with the old episcopal palace at Buckden in the time of a former Bishop of Lincoln. He confessed he had had a good many ups and downs in life, but I had no opportunity of discovering what they were, as, to my regret, he almost immediately afterwards left the works. It was difficult to get him into a communicative state of mind. One only hopes that if the episcopal sponsorship had failed to reach him in his wanderings, the fatherly advice he received on the following Sunday reminded him of old and better days.

The Sunday came in due course; the Mission flags

were floating from their exalted position at an early hour
in the morning.   The Bishop was at work by 10.30,
having left the house of his host at a little before 10.
During the day he preached in each of the chapels to
crowded congregations of railway folk of all classes and
types, from the bricklayer's hodman to the educated
engineer.   There were many present who, not owning the
luxury of a Sunday suit, were content to come in their
workaday dress.   On each occasion there was scarcely
standing room, and in the evening many were unable to
gain admission to the chapel, and were obliged to be content to stand outside and listen at the door or windows.
The services were hearty in the extreme, and the well-
known eloquence and intense earnestness of the Bishop
secured the profound attention of those who heard him.
In spite of the presence of a large number of " hobnailed "
boots, you might, to use a common phrase, have heard a
pin drop, and the eagerness of the faces upturned to the
preacher was enough to show what his words were doing.
The morning service at Wing was specially noteworthy, as
a Lay-reader (Mr. W. Chapman) was solemnly appointed,
in the presence of the congregation, to work among the
men at Corby, a Mission station nearer Kettering, where the
work had been carried on under the direction of the Rev.
B. E. W. Bennett, rector of the parish.   In his address,
the Bishop showed some of the various ways in which
the laity could, and ought to, aid the clergy in their
responsible duties; and while insisting on the Divine,
authoritative, and distinctive character of the office and
work of the clergy, he showed that for any true and
lasting success clergy and laity must work together in
one common cause, for one common Master.   He asked
for the help and support of those present in furthering
the Gospel which was now being regularly preached in
their midst.   The service concluded with the benediction

from the Bishop, who then returned to one of the huts
in which he had previously robed. He then left, and
had just time to get some refreshment at the Hall before
he started for his afternoon's work. Before three o'clock
he was at Seaton. Here he was accompanied by the
Chancellor of the diocese. We robed in one of the neighbouring huts, and went across the field to the chapel, but
it was with difficulty that we edged our way through the
crowded throng gathered in the chapel sometime before
the hour of service. Several had followed the Bishop
from the other end of the line where he had preached in
the morning, and were even present again at night. The
service was of the usual character, and the sermon was of
a thoroughly stirring nature, on the parable of the sower,
which was applied with subtle force to the varied circumstances of the congregation. The Bishop pointed out the
applicability of the parable to most of those present, telling
those whose duty it was to sow the good seed, that they
must look for fruit in the future ; and most earnestly exhorted the people to prepare their hearts for the reception
of the good seed, that it might bring forth abundantly. Any
mere summary of such a sermon is unsatisfactory, and
this clumsy attempt will give no idea of its force and power.
At the conclusion of this second service, his lordship
returned at once to Glaston, where he was announced
to preach a concluding sermon in the evening. This service
will be best described in an extract from one of the newspapers, which published an account of it the next week.

"In the evening the Bishop addressed the congregation at
Glaston, where the chapel was filled to excess, many people
being unable to get in. As this is the centre of the Mission,
and is commonly spoken of by the men as the 'Cathedral,'
and is the most populous station, he preached with special
reference to the character of the Mission, taking as his text,
'And when I saw Him, I fell at His feet as dead. And he laid
His right hand upon me, saying unto me, Fear not ; I am the

First and the Last: I am He that liveth, and was dead; and, behold, I am alive for evermore, Amen; and have the keys of hell and of death' (Rev. i. 17, 18). After speaking of the missionary career of St. John the Evangelist, he applied the words of encouragement, 'Fear not,' to the missioner whom he had sent amongst those to whom he was speaking. He showed further how those same words, from that same Voice, would also comfort and support those who were doing any work for God, in whatever capacity they were engaged on the Mission, and he exhorted one and all to acknowledge Jesus Christ as the First and the Last in all that they undertook, whether in Church work or in the silent and more hidden work of the individual soul. It need hardly be recorded that he was listened to throughout with the most rapt attention. At all the services large numbers of men were present, and the Bishop spoke of it as a gratifying fact; his words especially addressed to the young men anxious to do what was right and to bear witness for Christ, and yet surrounded and pressed sore by the temptations incident to the life of those living in large numbers in huts, and engaged on public works, will not easily be forgotten. He might have been a navvy himself, so graphically did he describe a young navvy's temptations. The well-known hymns selected for use at the services were joined in most fervently by all present. Those beginning, 'Art thou weary?' 'The Church's one Foundation,' 'A few more years shall roll,' 'I was a wandering sheep,' and the Old Hundredth Psalm, were sung with especial feeling. On the following day, the Bishop, accompanied by Mrs. Magee, the Mission staff, and some of the chief authorities on the works, made an excursion on the line towards Manton, in an open truck drawn by an engine. The party consisted of the Bishop, Mrs. Magee, the Lady Victoria and the Hon W. C. Evans-Freke, R. Stannard, Esq., C. J. Wills, Esq., P. N. Meares, Esq., Rev. D. W. and Mrs. Barrett, and the Rev. Leonard Addison. The various branches of the works were inspected, and the novel sight was witnessed of a Bishop going into the tunnel to see and talk to the navvy at his work in the bowels of the earth. He was most heartily welcomed all along the works, and many a rough hand grasped his with the feeling that he was a friend who had their best interests at heart. On the evening of the same day he received a deputation from the men, bearing an address from the representative members of the congregation, thanking him for the active interest he took in their welfare. Messrs. S. Hilling, H. Plowman, and H. Finch, were chosen as the deputation."

On the Tuesday the Bishop left us, and on his way
home went to a parish through which another new line
was passing, with a view, if possible, to organise a third
Mission there, he having previously inaugurated a similar
movement on the Nottingham and Melton line, of which
the Rev. J. C. Davies was appointed Chaplain.

The good seed which the Bishop sowed on this his
memorable visit bore its fruit in due course. The visit
not only tended to strengthen and consolidate the work
which had already been done, but we noticed afterwards many new faces at the service. Some of these
new-comers confessed that they had not attended the
services till then. Things went on steadily and quietly,
without much occurring to deserve special mention in
the way of great events, till the early summer of 1878,
when we were permitted to welcome our chief pastor
again; and this time for a special Confirmation. Before
giving an account of this, I must describe a remarkably
striking service at which his lordship was present on the
previous day. Our own district ended, as I have said,
on the confines of Gretton parish; but there were large
numbers of men working along the Gretton and Corby
section, who were mainly resident at a secluded spot
known as Corby Wood. Here the mission was conducted
by the Rev. B. E. Bennett and his zealous Lay-reader,
whose solemn appointment I have just mentioned at
Wing chapel in the previous year. As yet the Bishop
had not visited this section of the works, and when it
was announced that he would come one Wednesday afternoon in June, the men assembled at five o'clock to the
number of about three hundred, in their working dress.
It was a very striking sight to see them being brought
up literally in truck loads from the different parts of
the line. When the engine stopped they jumped out of
the waggons and ran across the field in which the huts

stood, in order to get a good place in the chapel, which
soon became so crowded that one end had to be taken
out in order that all might hear, as many were unable to
gain admission. It was amusing to see the swiftness
with which the men, suddenly imbued with the spirit of
church extension in a very literal sense, lifted out the
window frames and pulled down the end of the chapel
and made the boarding answer for a floor to the extended
portion. The service was opened with a hymn, and then
some suitable prayers were said by the Rev. B. E. W.
Bennett, and the Bishop's address followed. He spoke
with his usual earnestness and with the usual result
upon the minds of his hearers. He began his address
by showing in what respects he and his navvy friends
had very much in common, and thus he not only arrested
their attention, but gained at once their sympathy ; and
then he went on to tell them how their common but
higher aims might be advanced, and their common wants
satisfied, by bringing home most vividly the cardinal
truths of the gospel. He contrasted the lower and
animal life with the higher and spiritual one ; the
prodigal, the restless, the sinful life, with the life of the
settled and peaceful Christian, who, in the midst of this
world's changes, trials, and hard manual labours, placed
his hope and trust in Christ. The service lasted about
three-quarters of an hour. The men dispersed after
singing another hymn, some to their work, some to their
homes, all much encouraged by this truly Apostolic visit.
It was a literal going forth, as of old, into " the highways
and hedges, and compelling them to come in."

We have now to give an account of the Confirmation
at " our end."

Friday, 7th June, though a black letter day in the
Calendar, was certainly a red one in the history of the
Mission, for this made the fourth visit of the Bishop to

the works, and was a very solemn occasion in the history of some of the young people whom we had gathered in. The candidates from the works numbered twenty-six, and from the village thirteen. The service consisted of the Order for Confirmation and some hymns. The chapel was very full, a Confirmation on railway works being quite an attractive, and I venture to state, hitherto an unparalleled event. Many of the hut residents wondered what a Confirmation was. I remember when I gave a notice of it one Sunday evening a few weeks previously, and invited the unconfirmed to join the preparation classes, one young navvy came up to me after service and asked, in sober earnest, whether it was " a new sort of Penny Reading ! "

We are glad to be able to state that many of the candidates during the course of the next few weeks presented themselves at the highest of all our Christian services, the Holy Communion. They are scattered far and wide now, and all we can do for them is to pray and hope.

We have reason to know that most of our older communicants are steadfast in the faith ; let us trust that these younger soldiers of the Cross are fighting steadily too.

Besides this special Confirmation, candidates were prepared and presented at other times and from other districts on the line, but this occasion was so significant that it demands special mention.

The year, as we look back at our record, seems to have been rich in special occasions ; it remains for me to record two very interesting events which took place in connection with the Mission. The first of these was a remarkable service which was held on July 28th, in the Wing tunnel, which had just recently been finished.

" It was intended (to quote again the report of a local paper) as a thanksgiving for the completion of this section of the work without any serious accident.   There was a large number of people present, many coming in their working dress.   The service consisted of a short Mission form, supplemented by some popular hymns, the singing of which was most striking.   The harmonium was played by one of the miners engaged on the railway.   A sermon was preached by the Rev. D. W. Barrett, on the words 'What mean ye by this service?' (Exodus xii. 26).   After giving briefly a few precedents from Holy Scripture for services of a special character, and referring to the probability of even subterranean services, instancing the probable worship of the prophets hid by fifty in a cave, the witness of the 'dens and caves' in which holy men of old sought refuge, the history of the Catacombs —he went on to say, in some respects there were parallels and contrasts between the case of the Israelites in Egypt and that of the workmen engaged in the construction of that tunnel, *e.g.*, their occupation on public works, their different treatment, their deliverance from death, their exodus, their wandering in search of a new home, their duty of bearing witness in their wandering for the name and Church of their God.   He then showed how the service was intended to be one of commemoration, of thanksgiving, and instruction.   The congregation was most orderly and attentive."

Having described the former of these two interesting events, the narrative would be incomplete were an account of the second and still more striking service in Glaston tunnel omitted.   Here we will quote the words of a notice which appeared in the " Grantham Journal" which describes what took place.

" From time to time we have given our readers short sketches of the work of the Church amongst the railway men employed on the Kettering and Manton line in progress of construction through the county of Rutland.   The work at the Manton end is now approaching completion.   Last week, one of the tunnels over a mile in length—which passes one hundred and fifty feet beneath the parish of Glaston—was successfully bored through, and all the mining operations completed.   It was thought desirable that the event should be celebrated by a special service, before the workmen who had been engaged in it had left the scene of their labours for other railways. Accordingly, a short notice was issued, announcing that a special Mission service would be held in the tunnel on Sunday evening, September 8th, at half-past five, and that it was intended to be, as in the case of a similar gathering in Wing tunnel a few weeks before, a service of commemoration, thanksgiving, and instruction; and an earnest hope was expressed that the men would attend in large numbers. The invitation was accepted, and the whole hut population of Glaston and the neighbouring huts made the descent into the open ends of the tunnel, as well as nearly all the railway people living in the villages round, and large numbers besides flocked in from all quarters. Every class was well represented, from the engineers and agents down to the humblest navvy, miner, and bricklayer who had taken part in the work. It was computed by many who were there, and who were competent to judge, that there were no less than a thousand people present. Unfortunately, several heavy peals of thunder were heard towards evening, and the sky looked very black and threatening, and a great number of people turned back, fearing a storm was gathering, or there would have been many more. Happily the rain did not fall, and they who continued their journey reached the tunnel in safety, and were enabled to take part in this remarkable service. After penetrating some distance into the gloom, over the rough burnt ballast, the congregation approached the space in the tunnel where the service was to be held. This was lighted up with lamps hanging from the walls, and candles were also stuck upon them in the usual miner's candlestick of clay. The pulpit was a log of timber placed on a few bricks and the prayer desk an upturned wheelbarrow. A number of seats were arranged along the sides with a passage up the middle, but owing to their insufficiency, hundreds could not find room, and were obliged to stand. The service commenced with the hymn 'How sweet the Name of Jesus sounds!' This was followed by the order for a Mission service appointed by the Bishop for use in the diocese, containing psalms appropriate to the occasion. The selected lesson was Isaiah xl. verses 1-18, and was read by the Rev. and Worshipful W. Wales, the Chancellor of the diocese, and Rector of Uppingham. The latter part of the service, from the Apostles' Creed, was said by the Rev. J. B. E. Stansfeld. The clergy were habited in their surplices, which had a weird and striking effect in contrast with the deepening darkness of the long recess behind them. After the lesson, Bonar's grand hymn, 'A few more years shall roll,' was

sung with heart-touching solemnity, as they who sang it were standing between two spots where, a few months ago, two poor fellows
falling headlong down the shafts were suddenly summoned to
eternity. The hymn before the sermon was 'Art thou weary?'
The preacher was the Rev. D. W. Barrett, curate-in-charge of the
Mission, who took for his text, 'He brought me also out of the horrible pit, out of the mire and clay ; and set my feet upon the rock
and ordered my goings. And he hath put a new song into my
mouth. Even a thanksgiving unto our God. Many shall see it
and fear : and shall put their trust in the Lord' (Psalm xl. 2, 3, 4),
and was listened to throughout with earnest attention. After a few
introductory remarks, he first applied the words to the occasion
of the gathering that day, and pointed out some of the leading
thoughts of the text, speaking of the great danger, the merciful
deliverance, the joyful song, and the new life which should be the
result. At this point in the address, he called on the people to
make the walls of the very place where so many great dangers had
been undergone and deliverances effected, re-echo a better and a
holier song than they often had done in weeks gone by ; while
they stood now, and lifted up their voices in heartfelt thanks to
God in the words of the 'Old Hundredth Psalm.' The appeal
was responded to in a way which none who were there can easily
forget. When the hymn was ended, the preacher proceeded to
make the more spiritual application of the text, taking the same
chief thoughts to direct him in pressing home the danger of a life
of sin, the need of deliverance from it, and the happier and holier
life to which Jesus the Deliverer would lead, if only His guidance
were accepted, and the journey commenced anew on the 'narrow
way' leading to the eternal home. At the conclusion of the
sermon, the Mission hymn, 'I was a wandering sheep,' ended the
musical portion of the service, the harmonium being played by
Mrs. Kingston. A few appropriate collects were said, and two
special prayers were offered up, the first on behalf of those who
had been engaged on the works, and who were soon to be scattered
far and wide in the world, the second for the safety of those who
in future years should be called to 'pass by that way' in their
travels in pursuit of their lawful undertakings. The Rev. the
Chancellor then pronounced the benediction, and so a very solemn
yet joyful service terminated."

From this time the numbers of the men at work began
to grow less and less every day, and we must leave a

future chapter to describe the general exodus. As the hut population diminished, occasions for special services were more rare, and though the closing services at each of the chapels were days to be remembered, they cannot well be called red letter days. At each chapel special closing services were held, though there were but few of the railway folk left to attend.

A writer in the "Home Mission Field of the Church of England," the organ of the Additional Curates' Society which has so liberally furthered the objects of the Mission, after giving a short history of the work and describing the tunnel service, says—and his words shall conclude this chapter—

"With this scene, too, might fitly end our brief sketch of this most interesting Mission ; but perhaps a word or two should be added as to results. The question is often asked, when such work is described, 'What have been the results ?' Here, at any rate, they have been manifest. Evil livers have been reclaimed—men almost heathen brought to worship God—the young cared for and saved from evil influences. Enough, indeed, has been achieved to make those feel who have laboured here . . . that if they have sown the good seed with tears and painfulness, they shall doubtless behold the harvest-sheaves with joy and thankfulness. But it is a grave error to measure such works with results— the work is not man's but God's, and its real fruits are known to Him alone.

"This much is clear, that we have a plain and positive duty to discharge towards this much-neglected class of our fellow-countrymen. The navvy, let it be remembered, has been the pioneer of the great advance of civilisation which has followed from the wonderful engineering discoveries of this century. The navvy has greatly altered the face of the country, and the condition of many places which but for him would have been left far behind the age. As we reap the benefit of his labours, let us remember that these poor navvies have human hearts to be touched and immortal souls to be saved, as well as muscular frames and sinewy arms. The Church of England has a great work to accomplish amongst these men. May the hearts of English Churchmen be moved to enable her more and more fully to carry out the work ! "

CHAPTER IV.

LEISURE EVENINGS.

LEISURE was a word not much known on the Kettering and Manton Railway, and on many others too, I daresay, for the matter of that. Every other week the men were working on the " night shift;" but in spite of the " hurry scurry" of work, we contrived to spend a few happy evenings together every winter. The reading room attracted many most evenings, at all events for a little while, just to glance at the papers and enjoy a smoke after the evening meal. The " Stores," over which it was the duty of the reading-room keeper to preside, was often the trysting place of a studious little company at mid-day : the foremen and a few of the more intelligent liked to have a look at the papers as soon as they came in. Besides the attraction of the paper, our reading room in the evening held out other inducements to attend, in the shape of draughts, dominoes, and chess. One winter, smoking-hot coffee and buns might be had at a very moderate charge, at a little counter opening out from the room. The best remembered evenings will be the entertainment nights, when the dwellers in the huts from far and near came in crowds. We generally used to meet once a week two or three weeks previous to each of these gatherings for practice, and many of the workmen, their wives, " sweethearts," sons and daughters, figured valiantly, some as reciters, some as singers, some as readers ; and had we wished it,

we should have had no difficulty whatever in finding
those who could have produced on the stage some pleasing variations of the sailor's horn-pipe, the Scotch reel,
or even a veritable Irish jig. We had all sorts of material
ready to hand, not excepting those who had been

> "Soldiers, sailors,
> Tinkers, tailors"—

many of whom had travelled in many lands.

Just as we dispensed with the boisterous, so too we
found it was quite possible to conduct a thoroughly
popular entertainment without the *low* comic element.
Indeed, it was never seriously pressed, and never having
been served up, it was never missed, nor yet demanded.
It was very easy for a tolerably discriminate observer
and organiser to secure the adhesion of a few of the
more musical spirits, and to make the best of them.
The quiet fun, the quaint good-humour, and the attractive picturesqueness of the rehearsal-gatherings were
very refreshing and amusing after a hard day's work.
What was more, and this we had specially in view, they
brought many of us together in strong sympathy. The
numerous little failures, the "trys again," the slips of
memory, and at length the final triumph, as the task was
achieved of reciting ten verses "right up to the mark,"
learnt, perhaps, years and years before, all contributed
to make the memory of these practice-nights most
pleasing. Anyway, by the time the performers had to
stand up and face it out before the company, they
generally managed to get up their part as perfectly as
you could expect rough-and-ready amateurs' skill to produce : and by the kind and ready aid of musical and
literary friends from the surrounding villages, a series of
truly popular and useful entertainments was regularly
provided. On one occasion the entire entertainment

was undertaken by the members of the Mutual Improvement Society in a neighbouring town : for when once the better qualities and the higher tastes of the navvies became known, as well as the lower and less pleasing, the people round got to regard them in their true light, and united in trying to make their temporary residence a happy and an improving one. A word as to the manner in which we spent one of these leisure evenings may prove interesting.

Of course there was always an opening piece on the pianoforte, often accompanied by some other instrument ; and the programme was always well varied with glee, quartette, solo, duet, reading, and recitations, grave and gay. There was also the usual interval, when occasionally tea and coffee were served up to those who wished. Somebody, perhaps, will be inclined to ask whether there was not often a " shindy." No. Those who came did so with the intention of enjoying the evening after a hard day's work, and not " to make a row." Now, my dear railway folk, in the course of this little book I have often found fault with you, and I daresay some of you will add, " and served us right too ; " but I will say this for you before any man, that I have been to a large number of entertainments, Penny Readings, and cheap evening concerts for the people, but I have seldom seen such good behaviour at them as when I was amongst you. In six village readings out of ten anything but good order prevails. You know what very often happens. If you go to such an entertainment in many places, what will take place ? You will hear after every performer has resumed his seat, or even before he has had time to do so, a disgraceful series of unearthly yells, a chorus of shrill screeching whistles, and such a stampede with heels of boots vigorously thumping against the first hard substances they can reach, be it floor or seat, that the effect of the performer's effort is destroyed at once, and the drum of one's ear will be so unmercifully beaten as to be rendered incapable of much use for the next ten minutes. The whole place, in fact, is too often turned into a sort of " bear-garden." Now we had none of this; the " navvy " is too polite; and even had he desired to be troublesome, a committee of his brethren who were always ready to assist in making arrangements for these entertainments, would have informed him that his "room would be preferred to his company." The order was all that could be desired; instead of yelling, groaning, whistling, and shouting, you set yourselves to work (don't you remember ?) to give the performers a good honest round of clapping, and then addressed yourselves steadily to listen to the next " bit." Of course, if any of your favourites were announced, you received his name before even he began " to do his bit," as you called it, with a volley of claps, which gave him a little breathing space, and by the time he had squared his elbows, adjusted the ends of his gay necktie, cleared his waist-coat, hitched up his trousers, made the final tug at his watch-guard, inserted his thumb in the left-hand pocket of his waistcoat, and satisfactorily arranged himself, generally you were ready to a man. If any of the " little 'uns " came on to the platform to recite a simple poem, or to sing a " little ditty," you were all as still as mice. I daresay some of you who were there will not forget the hush which would steal over the audience as a child from the huts, with trembling accents and clear sweet voice, did his part, which, in addition to an extra round of cheers, brought forth the frequent ejaculation, " Well done, Nipper !" " Let's have another, young 'un!" and so on; all said in perfect good-humour and without noisy, clamorous uproar. The entertainments were not all of one type. Now a lecture on some popular

I

subject, now a Penny Reading; one night a magic lantern exhibition, sometimes a *bona fide* concert. Once or twice a negro entertainment was given, in one of the large workshops, by the engineers and clerks and others on the line. Here is a report of an entertainment of the character of which I have been speaking, which was given on the Nottingham and Melton Railway at Grimstone tunnel, where a Mission work similar to ours was being carried on :—

" At the commencement of these important works a number of the staff and minor officials thought it expedient that some provision should be made, whereby the workmen might be partially provided for without the aid of parochial relief in case of bodily sickness, or by accident overtaking them whilst engaged in the construction of the works. An institution was soon set in motion, which was heartily and readily acceded to by the men, whereby a given sum (though nominal) was stopped from each man's weekly earnings, which sum was supplemented by a grant of a percentage per head from the firm of Messrs. Lucas and Aird, who very readily fell in with the scheme, and congratulated the men on their prudence and forethought in endeavouring to provide and lay aside for a rainy day that which would be the means of securing medical attention and a comfortable living, without having to throw themselves upon the parish for sustenance whilst incapacitated from daily labour. Up to within a short time the fund has been self-supporting, but an unusual amount of sickness, accident, and death followed in rather quick succession, which brought a very heavy pressure on the funds of the institution, which finally ended in the balance being on the wrong side. The committee, not willing that the fund should die a premature death in consequence of the existing difficulties, resolved upon the happy plan of giving a series of entertainments, consisting of readings, songs, recitations, &c., which would not only tend to relieve financial affairs, but would also be amusing and instructive to the workmen, whose time after the labours of the day is somewhat monotonous, especially for those who are situated in the huts on the works. The last of these entertainments came off on Tuesday evening, in the drying shed on this tunnel, which place, with the help of many willing hands, has been rendered very comfortable for such occasions. Notwithstanding the inclement state of the weather, the room presented an animated appearance, a goodly number having assembled. The evening's proceeding took the form of a negro entertainment, given by the N. and M. Christy Minstrels, consisting of employées of the contractors, kindly assisted by several friends. It would be invidious to particularise individual merit; suffice it to say, that the whole of the performers did their utmost to make the affair a success, and, if we may judge from the frequent bursts of applause, their endeavours were not in vain. We may fairly say that, for an amateur party, they acquitted themselves admirably. These entertainments have entailed a large expenditure of time and trouble, but we trust that the efforts of the promoters may tend to the increased prosperity of the institution, and eventually lead to a balance in hand at the close of the operations."

Almost every week something or other was going on in the shape of wholesome entertainment at one or other centre of the works, and we were never without a very numerous audience. Often our proficients went to give help in turn in the villages round. The entertainments were not only numerous, but varied. Such variety was undoubtedly as pleasing to the men and their families as it was to the performers. These merry and happy nights drew us all together, and promoted unity, good-fellowship, and many other social virtues; and what was better still, they were often the means of bringing the workpeople together on the Sundays. They saw that the inside of the Mission rooms were bright, light, and cheerful, and discovered that they could spend a happy evening there on the week-day, and the consequence was, that very many were thus induced to try the experiment of spending a holy one there on the Sunday. What that experiment brought to hundreds they and their Maker alone can tell. We were thanked more than once or twice by the men for organising these entertainments, because they said that had they not been attracted to the Mission room on the week-day, they would never have summoned up courage to go there on the Sunday.

So these gatherings proved, indirectly, to be evangelising agencies. This is the reason they are recorded now.

Here would be a suitable place, if necessary, to speak of night schools and other such gatherings. Many very happy evenings were spent with the children, the dear navvy children, whose little faces are as bright and whose little hearts are as true as their brothers and sisters in towns and villages. How those youngsters, and their parents too, enjoyed the merry nights when Christmas-trees were provided for them! Fathers and mothers, and big brothers and sisters, were all admitted; and rare good fun it was. Altogether we had four such gatherings, and they will be remembered in after years by the children who swarmed in the Kettering and Manton Railway huts.

As we have already mentioned coffee as an attraction at the reading-room, it is only right to add that our Coffee Barrow, whilst it was efficiently worked, was a success. We were, however, unfortunate in our selection· of a manager, who did not continue to prove worthy of our confidence. There is no doubt that coffee-stalls placed at populous centres along a line, with an active boy to run up and down " the works " with supplies of refreshment, would prove very acceptable to the men. The choice of a clean, stirring, and *intelligent* manager ought to be an object of first consideration. You will be good enough to observe that I lay stress on the word intelligent, but I do not undervalue the other qualifications.

CHAPTER V.

A LETTER.

THE subject of this chapter may to the ordinary reader prove very uninteresting, not to say dull, but there are many of my old friends who, I believe, will read it with pleasure.   Scarcely a week passes but I receive a letter from some navvy friend wandering here and there.   Only this very day, on which I sit down to write these few lines, I have heard for the fourth or fifth time from a young navvy who is trying to do his best to serve his Master and be true to His Church, who tells me he finds it hard to do so amongst so many new faces and whilst making so many changes.   He has the same battle to fight in almost every place.   I have often been asked by the men to give them a copy of the following letter which I addressed to them a year ago.   By the kindness of the Navvy Mission Society ten thousand were distributed on the railway works of England and Scotland, but I am anxious that those navvy friends who possess this little account of their order, and of Church work amongst them, should be able to lay hands on my letter, which may serve as a reminder of our happy connection, and encourage them to keep to the good paths in which many of them have begun to walk.   Then, old friends, read it over again.   Here it is :—

MY DEAR BROTHERS AND SISTERS,—

   If you look at the end of this letter you will see who it is who writes to you. To many of you I am a stranger; but between hundreds of us, I hope and believe, a feeling of firm friendship exists,—a feeling, too, that we are members of the great brotherhood of Christ's Church on earth. Between us all, at any rate, there is this feeling, that we are members of the common brotherhood of humanity, which Jesus died to ennoble and to save.

Those of you who remember me as the Mission clergyman on the Kettering and Manton Railway—and, indeed, all—will, I am sure, at all events receive this letter kindly; but I pray that you will do more —that you will *read* it carefully. Read it when you are alone; read it to your mates round the cabin fire; read it to them as you sit down after your mid-day meal. May God grant it may remind you of the blessings He has in store for your soul. Let this letter call back to your minds, if you have forgotten them, the various conversations we have held together, the many happy hours we have spent in God's service in our little Mission chapels, and at the parish churches, and along the wayside, and even underground along the line. Not only so, but think of the words of counsel which have fallen from many others who have been working together with me for the good of your souls, and the glory of our Master. You are scattered far and wide now, up and down the land; some of you have gone away to distant shores; but I often think of you, old friends, and wonder where you are, what you are doing, and, above all, whether you are continuing steadfast in the faith, and true servants of our Lord. I rejoiced to know that many of you, when you were residing in this neighbour-hood, had some real and prayerful anxiety about your souls. I want you to listen now to me once more. You won't refuse, will you? Once more I say, read this letter. I venture to say, my men, its subjects, if not its actual words, are worthy of your thoughts. Landladies and mothers in the huts of England, won't you read it too? I think you will. When you have read it, hand it on to the lodger, and say, "Here's a letter from an old friend on Glaston tunnel, he has sent you a message; take it, and read it for your-self." Perhaps numbers of you will say, "I know nothing about Glaston tunnel, nor the man who writes the letter from there." But, my friends, I know something about you. "What is it you say you know about us?" is the answer you will give. Well, I will tell you. You are often painted a good deal blacker than you really are. Thoughtless people will have it that you are the blackest of the black. Now, I don't believe it. You may—some of you—have a rough exterior, but there are many warm and tender hearts among you. There are many among you who have spirits as gentle and souls as brave as are to be found in the higher ranks of life. But mind this, I don't say, and I don't believe, you are *all* so gentle and lamblike. There *are* black sheep in almost every flock, and there are some amongst you jet black. Brother, YOU who are reading this, are YOU one of the black sheep, are YOU one of the wandering ones, are YOU one who has left the fold of Christ? If you are *now*, I pray that you may soon be able to lift up your voice in the words of that hymn many of us have so often sung—

" Jesus my Shepherd is ;
    'Twas He that loved my soul,
    'Twas He that washed me in His Blood,
    'Twas He that made me whole;
    'Twas He that sought the lost,
    That found the wandering sheep ;
    'Twas He that brought me to the fold,
    'Tis He that still doth keep."

Don't you remember how lustily you sang those words when your friend the Bishop of Peterborough came to hold his special services among you ; and again down in the tunnel; you haven't forgotten them, have you ?

Well, then, this is certain, many of you are very black characters, but the Blood of Jesus will purify you. Many of you are wandering, but the Great Shepherd has a fold for you. Many of you are lost, but Jesus, the great Seeker, is looking for you. And oh ! happy and glorious thought, many of you are walking in the Light, and it will shine about you more and more unto the perfect day, when you shall rejoice in the light of heaven. These things I know about you. I know something else. You are outspoken men, and like to have things straight out and say what you mean. Sometimes it is in a rough sort of way, but it is honest all the same for that. *I am going to talk to you in an outspoken way.* If I understand *you*, and you understand *me*, we shall be on a fair footing. Old friends and new friends, I will tell you plainly why I am writing to you. We have a Father in heaven who loves us very dearly ; He hath a Son who died on the cross to save our souls from hell ; and there is, too, a Blessed Spirit whom that Holy Father and that Only Son hath sent to help us to lead a holy life. Oh ! I want you, too, to try and learn with me more of the power of the Father, more of the love of the Son, more of the help of the Blessed Spirit, every day of your lives, so that when the day of your death comes, you may be able to lift up your voices, though sickness may have made them weak and faint, and cry aloud with joy, "See what hath been done for my soul. 'Glory be to the Father, and to the Son, and to the Holy Ghost.'"

Now there are *three persons* in the Blessed Trinity, and there are *three seasons* in your lives, I want you to think about and see how you stand. Think of the Past, of the Present, and of the Future. One at a time. Let us begin with

I. THE PAST. I tell you what it is, brothers; this year of 1878 will soon be numbered with the past. The old church clock will soon strike twelve for the last time this year. Look back. You have seen what you call a "goodish bit of life" during the last twelve months. Some of you have been on the "Kettering and Manton," some of you on the "Dover and Deal," some of you on the "Northampton and Rugby," some on the "Banbury and Cheltenham," some in half a dozen other places. Well, what do you think about the year now gone? Has it been a *good* year for you, as you say, or not? Where have you spent it? Can you tell me? Think a minute. There's something more important than this—*how* have you spent it? God the Father has been very good to *you*, my brothers and sisters, in prolonging your lives, in showering upon you, though you deserved it not, blessings innumerable. How HAVE YOU SPENT IT? Look back! Don't you remember the time when you used to live at home under the old roof-tree in your father's cottage, within the sound of the bells of the dear old parish church, in the days before you took "to navvying," before ever you set a foot on public works? Don't you remember how different you were? You used to be seen at the church Sunday by Sunday, as it came round; what is more, you liked going, you were happy there. You used to pray when you were a lad, your heart used to warm up at the dear, sweet name of JESUS; but now, alas! this is altered. You have fallen away, you have got careless, you have gone from bad to worse, till you think it doesn't much matter what happens to you, as long as you've got enough to eat and to drink, a few shillings to help on a friend, and a shelter to cover you from the chilly winds of night. Oh! the memory of other and better days tells of the Father's goodness, but now you have lost the sense of His mercies. It is a long time, perhaps, you will have to travel over if you go back to the days of youth and childhood. I ask you to look back now through the year that is gone by; and I will give you here a few questions which I want you to put to yourselves. Now, *be fair; don't skip over the questions or the answers.* Here they are:

1. Have you prayed much to God during the year?
   *Answer*_____

2. Have you read your Bible very often?
   *Answer*_____

3. Have you been as often as you ought, or at all, to a place of worship?
   *Answer*_____

4. Have you or have you not made yourself like one of the beasts that perish by the sin of drunkenness?
   *Answer*_____

5. Have you been a swearing man?
   *Answer*_____

6. SISTERS, What about your lives, have they been the lives of Christian women?
   *Answer*_____

To one and all I say—think of the past. Many of you have run clean off the line to heaven. You were being drawn there, some of you, by the mighty power of God the Father's love, but you've uncoupled yourselves, and you are running back, down the incline to hell, with terrible swiftness; you are dragging others with you. Put on the brake, for God's sake! or you will be lost. Cry aloud to God as you stand and see the dangers you have been in, that you may be once more drawn back by the chain of love.

"Parson, you are too hard on us," I hear some of my friends say, "we are not all Sabbath breakers, not all drunkards, swearers, godless!" No, my men, you are not *all* so; within the hearts of many of you the love of God is deep. Many of you grieve at the excesses, the godless lives, of those among whom your lot is cast. Now let me ask *you* a question or two: Have you been the means of bringing any more souls to Jesus during the past year? Have you been bold in rebuking sin? Have you stood up like a man for Jesus when His Name has been dishonoured? What about your own soul? Have you nourished it by prayer? Have you fed it by thinking on God's Word? And, above all, have you sought to strengthen it in the Holy Communion of the Body and Blood of Christ? In short, the question that you and I, brothers and sisters, ought to put to ourselves, is this—Do we love our God better now than we did at the beginning of the year? Are we better Christian men and women?

If not, *why not?* There must be a reason for this. Pray this prayer: "*O God, my Father, have mercy upon Thy erring child!*"

II. THE PRESENT. I want this letter to reach you by Christmas Day. A happy Christmas to you all! How are you going to keep your Saviour's birthday? You won't stay at home all day, will you, and neglect the house of God? Are you going to waste your morning by rising late, and then loitering about till dinner time, and after that sit down and pass away the afternoon in merrymaking, and then, when evening comes, give way to idle dissipation? You won't do this, will you? Be merry, if you like, but with your merriment let not the name of Christ your Saviour be forgotten or be dishonoured. Oh! I should like to come to that hut and snatch the too oft-filled cup from your lips, and take you by the hand, and say, "Come with me, my brother, to the house of God, and hear what He hath done for your soul; come with me, and let us sing together the song which rang of old on Bethlehem's plains, 'Glory to God in the highest, and on earth peace, good-will towards men.'" Come and let us spend Christmas Day like Christian men, and learn to know more of the love of the Son of God, how He came down from heaven, how He took upon Him our flesh and became Man, and knew man's sorrows, man's temptations, man's griefs, man's weaknesses, man's sufferings here below. Let me entreat and implore you to think of the blessings of which this Christmastide speaks to you. The message to the shepherds was this: "Fear not, for behold I bring you glad tidings of great joy, which shall be to you and all people; for unto you is born this day, in the city of David, a Saviour, who is Christ the Lord." It is the message for *you*, too. Oh! go to the house of God, and hear more about this loving Saviour, Jesus, the Prince of Peace. That's your present duty. Now for

III. THE FUTURE. Oh! who dare look into the future of his life, and say what it will bring forth? God of His infinite mercy has spared our lives another year, to hear once again the blessed Christmas message. Before next year closes, many who read this letter may be dead.

"Days and moments quickly flying,
Blend the living with the dead;
Soon will you and I be lying
Each within his narrow bed."

Perhaps you will be killed suddenly by a fall of earth, by the blasting of a rock, by the crushing blow of an engine, by a bruise which may fester and mortify and poison the life blood, by a fall, by the slow torture of disease, or by the burning heat of fever. It may be

that you will die in some deep pit as yet unsunk ; in some cutting
as yet unknown, in some crowded hut as yet unbuilt, in some lone
cottage where yet you have never been, in some hospital where you
shall lie helpless on a bed of pain. But however it may be, or where
it may happen, let me ask you, Are you ready now ? Shall you be
ready to meet death then ? Soon you will wind your watches up
for the last time in 1878 ! and if you are thinking men and women,
you will say this ; Now 1878 is about over, what sort of person am
I going to be in 1879 ?*

For God's sake, who has made you, and for the Lord Jesus Christ's
sake, who has redeemed you by His precious Blood, and for the sake
of the Holy Spirit, who is ready to help you, oh ! let me pray you
to lead new and better lives.

Now if the past has a sad tale to tell, the present will bring before
you the means of lifting you up out of evil courses, and show you
where peace is to be found. What did the prodigal son, whom we
read of in the Gospel, do, after his life of wickedness, when the sense
of sin oppressed him ? He wisely and bravely, though in doubt and
trembling as to his reception, formed this noble resolution, "I will
arise and go to my father, and will say unto him, Father, I have
sinned against heaven and before thee, and am no more worthy to
be called thy son." That's my advice to you. Take the advice, and
God the Holy Spirit will help you to carry it out, and the angels of
heaven will rejoice that one more soul is brought back to the Father's
kingdom.

What sin is it which keeps you away from God? You have that to
conquer. I hope you will begin at once, if you have not done so
already. I hope, at any rate, as soon as the morning has dawned on
Wednesday, January 1st, 1879, you will have made up your mind to
say, From this time I will set to work to fight against the sin, and
henceforth JESUS shall be to me "the Way, the Truth, and the
Life." Brother Churchmen, brother Christians, fellow-sinners in
the homes on the public works of England, and wherever else you
may be, accept these words in the spirit in which they are written by

Your friend and brother,

D. W. BARRETT.

Glaston Tunnel, near Uppingham.

* It would be well perhaps, if, as you read this letter over again, you
were to put 1880 for 1879, and 1879 for 1878.

CHAPTER VI.

THE EXODUS.

"You know, sir, us chaps are just like them Israelites as you read of in the Bible," said a navvy to me one day, "we goes about from place to place, we pitches our tents here and there, and then goes on just like they did, only we don't hold together like as they did and all move on at the same time. I've thought how true that there hymn is as you has up at the chapel so often, 'I was a wandering sheep,' for it is just what we fellows are, and a good deal more foolish nor a sheep, some on us!"

This, then, is one necessary feature in navvy life, its wandering, roving, gipsy-like nature. A navvy wouldn't be true to his creed if he were not a wanderer; though many a hundred have become sick and tired of it, and would give almost anything to get settled. "If you only know'd what a job all this shifting is, master," was the frequent expression of the hut women, "you'd soon have had enough on it. My man has got that restless and roving that he can't stay in one place for long together, he's allus' a-wantin' to be on the move, and the sight of trouble and expense it is, nobody knows but them as has gone through w'it, and the expense, too, if he addles a bit now and agen, and gets a few pounds in the savings' bank, it's like a nothing when you comes to move, and is soon all goan when you are on the shift to a new job." As a body, my dear railway friends, I am afraid you are very much like, as you say, "Puffin' Billy," the steam-engine, when she's got the steam up—always ready "to go."

You don't stick at a job, *as a rule*, long enough to do
any good to yourselves. Of course you get the sack
sometimes, and then are obliged "to look out for
yourselves," but you more often "sack" yourselves by
that restless, uneasy spirit which you have cultivated.
Why can't you settle down a bit, man, when you come
to a fresh place, and say, Now I mean to stay on this job
as long as there is work for me to do, and give a fair
day's labour for a fair day's wage? Depend upon it, this
wandering about—a month in this place and a month in
that, a year here and six weeks there, a day and a
quarter on "this job," and a week on that—won't pay you
or the masters. I heard of a man coming into a hut a
short time ago on a Tuesday, bringing his wife and family
with him, and turning out on a Friday. To what extent
these wanderings were carried on you will scarcely credit,
unless you are one of the men themselves. I have
conversed with men who have worked in almost every
county in England, and in many foreign countries too.
Mrs. Charles Garnett, whose efforts to better the condition
of the navvy are so well known, gives in a very interesting paper in the Sunday Magazine the history of a navvy,
written by himself, which is so very characteristic that I
cannot resist the temptation to quote it.

"——was born in Oxfordshire in 1832. His mother died when
he was six years old. There was no school in the village and he
had to go to work, and he did not know a word of his book when he
was ten years old. There was a railway started not far off, so he
and another made it up to go. They made a start, but did not
succeed ; so they had to come back. After that he went into service for two years, and then went for a soldier and went abroad,
came back, and after being at Portsmouth, Woolwich, Deptford,
Aldershot, and Dover, got discharged at Dover, and started to
work at Dover Heights. There was a church, but he never went
After being there for some time, left and went to Canterbury, to
Rotoum, and Maidstone ; was not there long before he left and went
to Plumstead ; there was no school or church there (for navvies).

Went from there to Battersea Fields, through London to Kew Bridge; no school or church there. From there to Hounslow, Maidenhead, High Wickham, to Oxford, Banbury, Nottingham, Leicester, Rugby, Alperton, Clay Cross to Shrewsbury, Herne Bridge; no church or school there. On from there to Bridge-north, Worcester, Malvern to Gloucester, Cheltenham to Salisbury, Gosport, Portsmouth, past bridge (?). No school, nor church there. From there to Battersea and Mussel Hill, Bramford, Croydon, Horsham and Guildford; no school, no church there. From there to Dartford, Gymford (?) Bat and Ball. No church, no school there. Then to Herne Bay, Ramsgate, down to Dover. No church, no school. Next to the Isle of Grain to Cliff. No church and no school. Then to Belham, Croydon Common; no church, no school. Next to Shoreham and Afford (?). There was a church at Afford. I had used to go every Sunday. Was there a good while. Was sent to Tunbridge. There was a church, but I seldom went. From there to Hampton Court, to London, Newington Causeway. After being about London, the Isle of Dogs, took the boat at London Bridge to Hull, to Beverley, Market Drayton to Doncaster, York, and then to Sherborne, to Leeds, Halifax, Wisington (?). To Castle-Carr, Flyflat, Barden Moor, then to Bradfield Dale. There was a Scripture-reader there that used to come and read of a night in the huts, but there was no school or church. From there, back to Barden Moor. There was a school for the children on Sundays, and there used to to be a preacher come on Sunday nights. From there to the Strange, to Dewsbury, Crow's Nest. From there to Whitworth. There was a church there, but I never went. From there to Lindley Wood. From there to Tintwistle. There was a church there, I went very near every Sunday. From there to Ashton, Guybridge, Nuten (?) Wood. No church or school. Then to Distey (?). No church or school there. To Chewbent and Manchester, Rochdale back to Whitworth. From there to Riponden, near Sowerbridge. No church, no school there. To Holmforth, Blackamore Foot and Deer Hill, Oxenhope, Lisher, Lancashire Moor, Ponden, Harndel, Pulbro', Little Hampton, Medhurst, and Pedeth (?). To Bristol, old passage. To Andover, Salisbury Cross, Salisbury Plain, to Devises and Hungerford, Chippenham, Cane (?), Malborough, Kigton (?), through the forest down to Hereford, Brecon. There was no church nor school at none of these places. Then on to Blackheath, to Stourbridge and Bromeham, to Hilltop. No church or school at none of these places. From there to Oxford, to Tame. No church or school was there. From there to Sevenoaks, then away through

London. Then away to Dudley, Chapeldreft (?) to Budeley, Tenby, Severn Valley. No church or school none of these places. Away then to Worcester and Malvern. No church, no school there. Then to Salisbury, and took right across there till I got to Wisendon. No church, no school there. I can safely say that on a Sunday when I have been at some of these places, I have wished 'twas Monday morning to go to work, but since *I have been at Lindley Wood, I have wished it was Sunday.*"

This will give a tolerably accurate idea of the navvy's roving life, though hundreds wander much further afield than this. This is what the majority of those who left the Kettering and Manton were doomed to do, partly by their own choice, and partly from the nature of the life they had chosen. Whence they came one hardly knew, and where they went was an equal puzzle. It was the trying part of our Mission work to say good-bye to those in whom we had learned to take an affectionate interest, and, literally, to see them start for a pilgrimage up and down the wide, wide world. I wonder how many thousands of different men worked at different times on our line. This would puzzle the acutest statistician. The scene could only be compared to a sort of kaleidoscope, in which the changing colours were human beings. Hundreds of the men were like fish, and kept going up and down the stream winding through the district, and had a nibble here and a nibble there, and never seemed satisfied. As a working man said to me one day, " These chaps will hang themselves on their own hook some of these days."

Well, these changes were continually going on, and prepared one's mind for the gradual exodus to which I have referred. The works may be said to have been at their height from June 1877 to June 1878; from this latter time, till the close, there was a constant cessation of work taking place. The huge gangs of seventy or eighty now by degrees grew less and less. First, perhaps, they were reduced to one-half, then to a third, till at

length they disappeared altogether.   The cutting which but
a few weeks before had presented a scene of busy life was
now almost deserted, and there were only to be seen two
uninterestingly smooth banks, with two dreary lines of
metal stretching between them, and perhaps a solitary
individual sowing grass seed from a basket slung upon
his arm, without even the heart to whistle as he plied his
lonely task.   That bridge, which viewed from a distance a
year ago looked as though it were a parapet wall being
scaled by a company of brave warriors after a heavy bom-
bardment, now looks like what it is, a very neat, trim and
naked red-brick bridge.   It looks so dull and cheerless
that one has hardly the heart to watch the remaining
mason who is giving the pointing a finishing touch.   If
you go and stand at the end of a short tunnel you can't
see so much as a human being; the only sound you can
hear is the water dripping from one of the numerous tiles
in the walls.   You might shoot a cannon through it and
hit nobody, whereas had you done so a twelvemonth ago,
you would probably have scattered a crowd of men and
a score of scaffolds in all directions.   Proceeding a little
farther, you still meet with evident signs of the closing
scene.   Look at yonder group of huts.   A few months
since the smoke might have been seen curling from every
chimney, a group of merry children playing round every
door, and the hum of many voices heard within.   Now every
other hut, and sometimes five or six in succession, are
tenantless.   The windows are broken, the chimneys removed; broken bedsteads, stools, tables, and empty beer
barrels piled in reckless confusion near the door, testify
that the occupants have "flitted and gone to another job."
There, by the bank side, were half a dozen as cosy little
nooks as you might well wish to see in a day's tramp,
now they are every one gone, a few brickbats, some
broken bottles, half a dozen boards papered with pictures

from the "British Workman," or the "Gospeller"—an old "Graphic," with the "Police News" peeping out behind, three or four bars from the kitchen grate, and a heap of sods are about the only vestiges left. Most of the ground has been levelled and the grass has begun to grow. So all along from end to end these evidences of departing activity appeared most depressingly. One day an engine was despatched to other works, another, a load of "plant," the next, a few spare huts, and so on. Day by day the place became still more dull, and a sense of loneliness stole over one, amounting almost to the depression of solitude; one seemed almost inclined to go and talk to the rusty old engine which has tugged many and many a ton of earth up through one of the shafts. The "loco," too, which often saved me many a long drag over hill and valley now stands silently in the shed; "her" great throbbing pulse is silent, "her" faithful friend and driver, "Scotty," is gone. You might walk a mile along the tunnel top and hardly meet a soul. So this exodus began and went on, and soon the whole navvy tribe will have left the neighbourhood, and some of the neighbours, no doubt, will be heard to exclaim, "A good thing too!" Perhaps so, in some ways, but they will have lost many a true friend among the "wandering tribe," and many a one will, perhaps, have joined the ranks. From the navvies I know many a thought will be turned, in years to come, to the hills and dales of Rutland. For one, my thoughts will often go back there. I hope this simple narrative will cause the countryfolk and others where our railway-makers go, to think in future more kindly of our navvy friends, and even of their failings, and that they will be received wherever they go as men, and act themselves as true men should. The last six months of our Mission work among them was a most trying time, though most encouraging,—trying, to say

K

"good-bye" to so many a newly-found, though true, friend; encouraging, to know that when the "good-bye" came, there came with it many a time an oft-repeated expression of gratitude that God had thrown us together as pastor and people. Often has the pressure of the rough hand of the working man, the trembling accents of his voice, and the tearful eye, as we spoke our few last words together, told me that the working man's affections, his better self, can be won over to Christ. During these months it was almost a daily duty to part with various members of our congregation. We scarcely know now where to turn our thoughts and not find ourselves thinking of old friends. Some are sleeping their long sleep in many a quiet village churchyard of the country in which we met and worked together. Others, nearly all now, are scattered far and wide, north and south, east and west: some in India, in the British Islands and Colonies, in New Zealand, in Canada; all over the wide world they are roaming. May God protect their going out and coming in! How far He has blessed the effort of the Church to reclaim her wandering children, none can tell. We do not care to count up the numbers brought in, or to tell of results. We could not do it if we wished. Our Master has said, Watch, work, wait, and pray. In spite of hundreds of failures, we have been happy in our work; seed has been sown by many sowers—from the chief pastor of the diocese downwards: the great Harvest alone will show the fruit, what it is, whether it be much or little. My railway friends who read this will, I hope, bear in mind that, though severed now by distance, our hearts shall be true to one another, and though parted now, we look, after we have travelled over the great highroad of life in the world, for a reunion, when our place of gathering will be no longer a shifting tabernacle, but a Temple "not made with hands, eternal in the heavens."

APPENDICES.

APPENDIX A.

NAVVY MISSION SOCIETY.

A DRAWING-ROOM MEETING to forward the objects of this Society was held on the 16th of May at the Earl of Aberdeen's house in Upper Grosvenor Street. The Bishop of Ripon presided, and the speakers were the Bishop of Peterborough, the Dean of Ripon, the Dean of Chester, the Earl of Aberdeen, Sir H. Verney, and the Secretary of the Mission.

The Bishop of Ripon in opening the proceedings remarked that this Society had been formed to meet a special want, to minister to the needs of a migrating class, to establish schools, services, and means of religious and social improvement in all navvy settlements. Until this Society was formed, efforts were made in only a few places for the good of the navvies, and at all the rest they were left entirely neglected. Out of thirty-six settlements, only three had schools, and four, services, and yet the navvy population of England alone cannot be less than sixty thousand souls. Navvies gladly welcome opportunities for social and religious improvement, and in his lordship's own diocese he had seen the happy result of such efforts.

The Bishop of Peterborough said : " I am deeply interested in the success of this Society, for, from personal experience, I know the needs which the Bishop of Ripon has alluded to, to be very real. A railway was to be made in my diocese, and suddenly four thousand new inhabitants were hutted in temporary villages in rural parishes. The clergy of these parishes—already fully occupied, were unable to do anything. Besides, navvies are a peculiar class, somewhat like gipsies in their isolation, and requiring special arrangements and special workers. I appointed a chaplain, ... and under him were employed Scripture-readers. I myself directed the Mission. The contractors built three wooden churches at different points, and there I have preached to the most earnest and attentive congregations. Committees of the men at each place gave their assistance, and I was struck by their manly respectable appearance. The following day I received many a warm grasp from hands clay-stained and oily, which I there had seen handing books and directing friends to seats." His lordship then spoke of the good results of this now ended Mission.

The Dean of Ripon said : " I ought to know something of railway life, for I was volunteer chaplain for four years upon a line of railway which was made twenty years ago through my parish in Buckinghamshire, by Mr. Brassey. Finer or more warm-hearted fellows than the navvies I never met with, ever ready to do a kindness, and most grateful for any shown to themselves. Their improvement was rapid and marked. Mr. Brassey was obliged by law to employ a certain number of policemen, but he said to me, ' There has been little need of them, for your scripture-readers have done *their* work.' " The Dean added that the Navvy Mission desired to second and organise local efforts ; it had suffered a great loss in the death of its single-hearted secretary, the Rev. L. M. Evans, and he earnestly appealed to those present to aid its work by forming local committees, collecting funds, and in the neighbourhoods where navvies were working, by taking a personal interest in the men. They would always meet with a courteous reception. A lady of whom he heard, visited the navvies to read to them, and was gladly welcomed ; she never heard any rough words, for after she had been twice or thrice, one of the gangers called sixty of the men together and said, " Now, lads, this little thing is trusted to us, and we must never let her hear anything she wouldn't at home."

The Dean of Chester said, when he was a boy little was known of navvies, but they had even then done so much pioneer labour that the canal which brought coals to near his north country home was called " The Navvy." To navvy labourers we owe docks, roads, water-supply and drainage ; and this Society, which, following their migrations over the country, sought to bring them nearer to God, and to raise their social condition, had his warm approval.

The Rev. J. Cornford (Ripon), Secretary of the Mission, said that so rapid had been the demands for help from the Society, that though he held in his hand urgent appeals from different parts of the country, —all of which of necessity had been refused,—and though, when he became secretary, four months ago, there was in hand a balance of £170, the Society was at the present moment *without funds.* He would thankfully receive subscriptions, and also books, new or old, for lending libraries, Bibles, night-school books, maps, &c.

The Earl of Aberdeen said both the Bishop of Ripon and the Bishop of Peterborough had thanked himself and the Countess for lending these rooms on this occasion, but he must rather thank his lordship for presiding, for with regard to the navvies he felt himself a learner to-day; he took much interest in the subject of the employment of railway men, but he could not forget that navvy hands formed the lines themselves, and he wished this admirable Society every success.

Sir H. Verney begged also to thank the Bishop of Ripon for presiding that day. Dean Fremantle had referred to the time when a railway was made near Claydon. Then it was that personally he made the acquaintance of navvies, and he must bear testimony that instead of being a nuisance, they were a benefit to the neighbourhood; nearly five thousand were employed, and at that time a French invasion was reported, and they told him if he worked to raise a regiment, one thousand of them were ready to enlist. So large a number of persons left uncared for in a rural district might no doubt give trouble, but the opposite result had been the experience in theirs, and he thought the blame of the lawlessness with which navvies were credited did not always justly lie with the men alone. Abroad he had seen the results of care and neglect. On one line, constructed by Mr. Brassey, he found the men respectable, steady, and universally liked. Upon another where the navvies had no Sunday services, reading rooms, &c., they were drunken and disreputable, and made the name of Englishmen a terror.

The proceedings terminated by the Bishop of Ripon pronouncing the benediction.

APPENDIX B.

PRESENTATION TO THE BISHOP OF PETERBOROUGH.

A paragraph in "The Guardian" for July 2, 1879, gives an account of a presentation to the Bishop of Peterborough.

An interesting event took place the other day. It was spontaneously suggested by one or two of the workmen still left, that it would be right that they should acknowledge by some little gift what the Bishop had been the means of doing for them. Accordingly a collection was made amongst the "old hands" who had been on the work some time, and a small but handsomely bound Bible was sent to his lordship, with a few homely but sincere words of gratitude written on a sheet of paper inside.

April 28, 1879.

THE RIGHT REV. LORD BISHOP OF PETERBOROUGH.

Will you kindly except this Bible as a token of respect from a few of the old Hands left on the Kettering and Manton Railway as we feel we should like to make some acknoglement for the great Intrest you have taken in our Spiritual Wellfare.

We think as Railway Men it tis a great Honour for a Bishop to Come Amoung us all Much More to take the Intrest you have done we all Sinceley thank you for having a Mission Amoungest us which we hope will be a blessing to Many of us and we Sincerley hope you will not reget for what you have done

Signed on behalf of the Congegrations work man

S. H——.

H P——.

The Bishop has sent the men the following reply, which shows the relation existing between him and them, and augurs well for future efforts of the Church amongst her neglected children employed in making our various lines of railway :—

THE PALACE, PETERBOROUGH,
June 23, 1879.

DEAR FRIENDS,—I thank you heartily and gratefully for the Bible you have given me, and for the kindly words with which you have accompanied your gift.

When three years ago I proposed to set on foot a Mission for the navvies of the Kettering and Manton line, I felt sure of two things. One was, that you to whose labours we owe so much of our convenience and comfort had the strongest claim upon us for any services we could render you in return. The other was, that we could render you no truer service than that of bringing within your reach the blessings of the Gospel and Kingdom of Christ.

I was very hopeful, too, as to one thing more, namely, the reception which you would give to the missioner whom I might send you. I was persuaded that if I could only find for you a loving and faithful minister, you would welcome him as one who had come amongst you to care for your souls, and that you would erelong give him real and efficient help in his labours.

The result has fully justified my expectations. You have welcomed and helped your missioner readily and warmly, and his loving and earnest efforts have been largely blessed of God to your good.

The help that I could give him and you in this work was comparatively small, but it was gladly given, and the warm expression of
your thanks for it more than repays it, in the encouragement it gives
me to like efforts in the future and in the new and deep interest it
gives me in navvy work and missions. I shall never hear or read of
Mission work amongst navvies without its recalling to me the pleasant
hours that you and I have shared together, or without its prompting
me to pray for God's blessing and guidance on those engaged in that
work, and on the souls whom they may bring to the knowledge and
the love of our Lord and Saviour.

Believe me, my dear friends, your faithful friend and servant
in Christ.

W. C. PETERBOROUGH.

To MR. S. H—— & H. P——
On behalf of the Congregations of the Manton and Kettering Line.

APPENDIX C.

The need of special efforts for the spiritual welfare of the men is
pressing. The annexed statement of the Secretary of the Navvy
Mission Society, showing the number of works in progress early in
1879, will be read with interest.

* Large Works; † small ones. S R stands for Scripture Reader.
N S, Night School. R R, Reading Room. S, Service on Sundays
S S, Sunday School. D S, Day School.

RAILWAYS—* Manton and Kettering, 3 S, 3 S S, 2 R R, 2 D S.
     2 N S.—Rev. D. W. Barrett, Mr. Bruster, and others
 ,, * Northampton and Rugby, S R, 2 S, 2 S S, N S.—Rev. C.
     Yate and Rev. W. L. Mackesy
 ,, * Eastbourne and Tunbridge Wells, R R, S, S S, N S.—
     J. Firbank, Esq., Rev. J. Ley
 ,, * Dovercourt, R R, C R, S.—S. Ridley, Esq.
 ,, * Metropolitan District.—Messrs. Lucas and Aird
 ,, Banbury and Cheltenham, R R, S.
 ,, * Dover and Deal, S R, S, D S, S S, R R.—T. C. Walker, Esq.
 ,, * Northampton and Bletchley.—Mr. Nelson
 ,, Corby and Gretton, S R, S, S S, R R, D S.—Rev. B. E.
     Bennett, Rev. L. Addison, and Mr. W. Chapman
 ,, † Barton Boss & Cross Lane, R R.—Mrs. C. Bell

RAILWAYS.—† Stourbridge
,, † Ryde New Line and Pier.—T. M. Penn, Esq.
,, † L. B. & S. C. R. Extension, S R.
,, † Acton Railway ⎫
,, † G. W. Extension ⎬ Hon. Miss Kinnaird
,, † Halesworth and Southwold.—Rev. F. F. Noott
,, † Severn Bridge
,, † Dewsbury Railway
,, † Manchester and Redcliffe, and S. D. Railway
,, Ely and Bury St. Edmund's
,, G. N. and L. & N. W. R. Joint Lines
,, Melton and Nottingham.—Rev. J. P. Davies
,, Steeton and Keighley
,, N. E. South Shields
RESERVOIRS—* Barden Moor, S R, S, 2 S S, 2 N S, 1 D S.
,, * Audenshaw, Manchester, S R, S, S S, N S.—Rev. A. C.
   Balkeley, Mrs. Cosgrave
,, * Colwell, S R, S, S S, D S, R R.—Rev. C. Bird and W.
   Rigby, Esq.
,, * Denshaw, S R, S, S S, N S, R R.—Rev. H. Heppinstall
,, † Crown Brook
,, * Bill o' Jack's, S S, D S.—Rev. J. Cheetham (Greenfield)
,, Cleveland W. W., Skelton
,, Cockermouth
,, Copster Hill
,, Spring Mill, Broadley
,, Ilkeston
,, Wissenden Head
,, Abbeystead, Lancaster
,, Bridgewater
,, South Staffordshire
,, Buxton
,, Llanelly
,, Brentford
,, Hampton
,, Hednesford
  († †)
,, Fewston, S R, 2 S, 2 S S, 2 N S, 2 R R, 1 D S.
,, † Harrogate
DOCKS, &c.—** Victoria Docks, S R.—Rev. H. Bodily and Hon. Miss
   Kinnard
,, * Holyhead Docks

Docks—* West Hartlepool Docks
,, * New Slipway, Penarth Docks.—Rev. C. Parsons
,, Brading Harbour.—Rev. J. Le Musurier
,, * Hampton, W. W.
,, † Brentford ,,
,, Sutton Docks
,, Newcastle Docks
,, Barrow-in-Furness Docks
,, Grimsby Docks
,, Hammersmith Docks
,, Hull Docks
Drainage—† Buxton
,, † Glen Sluice, Spalding
,, Horsham Sewerage, S, S S.
,, Newton Heath Sewerage, Manchester
,, * Peterborough Sewerage
,, * West Kent Drainage, S R, S.—Miss Gladstone
,, * Basingstoke Drainage.—G. Middleton, Esq.
,, Chesterfield Drainage
,, Denbigh Drainage
,, Camborne Drainage
,, Stourbridge Drainage
,, Skegness Drainage
,, Hammersmith.—Hon. Miss Kinnaird
,, Sewage Farm, Mitcham
,, Winchester Main, R R.—Miss Perks
Various—York Barracks
,, Gas Works, New Bradford
,, York Cattle Market
,, Ripon, Studley Ponds
,, Esplanade, Southend
,, Liverpool Docks, Roads, &c.—Miss Birrell.
,, Silverdale Sea Wall, S.—Rev. J. L. Pain.

The very existence of these works will speak for itself, and tell of the thousands of men who must be employed in their construction.

The late Secretary of the Navvy Mission Society makes the following eloquent appeal in the pages of the "Quiver," to which I call your attention. He says:

"The last of these 'remarks' which I will quote is—

'Sir,—We have been here nearly four years, and we have never been visited by any minister. Our job is nearly finished. No one has ever so much as sent us a tract to read on a Sunday.   THE MANAGER.'

"I said I would claim my reader's sympathy for navvies on the ground of facts; and surely this one fact, even if it stood alone, would be sufficient ground. But we have seen already that it does not stand alone. It is merely a description, plainer and more outspoken than usual, of the state of things in many places.

"If, then, these things be so, the question is, Can anything be done to mend matters? What can be done? and to whom must we look for the doing of it? One very common reply to these questions is, 'Let the clergy of the several districts in which these navvies are look to it; let them provide all that is needed—services, schools, and so on—for the use of these people, who are their parishioners, if only for a time.' This sounds plausible enough, and there are cases in which all this can be done, and is done. But imagine a case—such as I have seen—of a large district with a dense population and a small, over-worked staff of clergy. The centre of the parish, in which dwell five-sixths of its whole population, is a manufacturing town, but the parish boundaries stretch far away, and enclose distant moorland hamlets and large tracts, it may be, of almost uninhabited country. Into one of these outlying districts come the navvies. There within the boundaries of the parish, but perhaps four or five miles from the town, is formed the navvy village, requiring a parochial organisation of its own.

"In many cases the old saying holds good, that everybody's business is nobody's business. There is no lack of people to cry shame on the neglect which the navvies suffer, and to say, 'Something ought to be done for these people!' The difficulty is to find those who say, 'This is my business; I must do something for them!'

"Generally speaking, the responsibility is very widespread. Wherever a large number of navvies is gathered to execute some extensive public works, there is sure to be a large number of people who derive benefit from their presence. In the first place, their employers are benefited. Then the neighbouring landowners, on whose property the works are executed, derive pecuniary advantage. The tradesmen, too, of the neighbouring towns and villages profit largely, for the navvies spend their earnings freely. On all these there rests directly some share of responsibility. And indirectly it spreads wider still. If the works are of public utility, then on the public in general falls a share of the burden, and to each and all of us belongs the duty of seeing that, so far as we may, the men who make our railways, our reservoirs, our docks and harbours, are not uncared for in the things which concern their souls."

APPENDIX D.

In addressing the annual meeting of the Additional Curates' Society in London during the present year, the Bishop of Peterborough, in urging the claims of the Society, is reported to have spoken thus :—

" Now turn with me to quite another part of my diocese. From the great towns and manufacturing districts, turn with me to some quiet quarter of my diocese that is invaded by a great mass of navvies.

" In the midst of such quiet country parishes picture to yourselves 4000 men, women, and children poured into a few of them—a great invading mass which must be invaded, if we could successfully do it, with all the force of Christian love and of Christian zeal, to win them over to the service of their Heavenly Master. We talk sometimes of this great mass employed on our railway works—these great congregations of men and women ; we talk of them as if they were the difficulty of the Church and the danger of the nation ! And so they are, but they are something else ; they are the wealth of the Church and the strength of the nation when really won for God and for Christ. The riches of the Church are the human souls which she gathers to her ; when she possesses them she is rich in the divinest riches. Picture to yourselves, then, the country pastor who has to encounter these multitudes gliding past as if they were foreigners ; and who, knowing nothing of their tongue, would be dazed and bewildered to find some way in which to reach them before they passed away. We need quickly to pour upon them a trained, ready, zealous, powerful agency, especially suited to the work. And here there is another work for our Society."

| Monthly, 6d. | | Volumes, 3s. 6d. |

MISSION LIFE;

OR,

HOME AND FOREIGN CHURCH WORK.

CONTRIBUTORS.

BISHOP OF ANTIGUA.
BISHOP OF AUCKLAND.
BISHOP OF BALLAARAT.
BISHOP OF BARBADOES.
BISHOP OF DUNEDIN.
BISHOP OF GUIANA.
BISHOP OF HONOLULU.
BISHOP OF HAITI.
BISHOP OF MARITZBURG.
BISHOP OF PERTH.
BISHOP OF RUPERTSLAND.
BISHOP OF PRETORIA.
BISHOP OF SASKATCHEWAN.
DEAN OF PERTH.
ARCHDEACON OF VANCOUVER.

ARCHDEACON OF COLOMBO.
Canon CHURTON.
Canon G. H. WILKINSON.
Canon WARE.
Hon. and Rev. W. H. LYTTELTON.
Rev. S. J. STONE.
Lady FREDERICK CAVENDISH.
Lady STUART HOGG.
Hon. Mrs. J. G. TALBOT.
Earl NELSON.
Sir ROBT. HAMILTON.
Sir BARTLE FRERE.
Sir CHARLES NICOLSON.
&c.   &c.   &c.

OPINIONS OF THE PRESS.

" We cannot too cordially commend it. It is the most trustworthy and interesting of our Missionary Magazines."—*Standard.*

" Very interesting. Vastly different in every way from the dreary missionary records in which the wearied ' Sunday readers ' of thirty years ago sought refuge. Happy the new generation, as far as Sunday is concerned."—*Spectator.*

" A well-edited repository of news from every part of the Mission Field."—*Nonconformist.*

" Gives interesting information about missionary doings of a sort which we rarely see elsewhere."—*Record.*

" You cannot open it anywhere without seeing that in style and interest it may fairly compete with any of the magazines. Its goodly row of volumes make up a missionary library, which for extent of subject, breadth of view, cultivation of style, and general attractiveness, far exceeds anything that has been attempted in this line before."—*Guardian.*

" A Publication which deserves to be better known. It breathes a broader and more liberal spirit than is often apparent in professedly religious magazines."—*Graphic.*

LONDON : W. WELLS GARDNER, 2 PATERNOSTER BUILDINGS.